The Former Alt House

Biography of a Nagasaki Landmark

Brian Burke-Gaffney

For Lane R. Earns
friend and colleague

CONTENTS

Introduction

The historic theme park Glover Garden opened in Nagasaki in September 1974, a time when Japan was basking in unprecedented economic growth. Nagasaki had finally emerged from the shadow of the atomic bombing, revived its traditional shipbuilding and fishing industries, and found a lucrative new source of revenue in tourism. Thousands of people were flocking to the city, not just to visit the atomic bomb museum and Peace Park, but also to revel in the romantic afterglow of centuries of international trade and cultural exchange.

A decade earlier, a group of entrepreneurs In Aichi Prefecture had established a theme park called Meiji Village to preserve nineteenth-century Western-style buildings facing destruction under the wave of development rushing across Japan. Having noticed the potential for a similar tourist attraction, the Nagasaki municipal government unveiled Glover Garden, showcasing former foreign residences and several Meiji-Period buildings relocated from other parts of the city.

But a fundamental difference set Meiji Village and Glover Garden apart. While Meiji Village was a museum of obsolete buildings dismantled and reassembled on an open plot of land in the countryside, Glover Garden was located in Minamiyamate, the hillside residential district of the former Nagasaki Foreign Settlement. Most of the gracious villas on the hillside had been abandoned by their Euro-American inhabitants prior to World War II, but they remained largely intact, hidden under the shade of towering camphor and ginkgo trees, snuggling behind walls overtaken by bougainvillea and banksia rose vines.

The former Glover House and former Ringer House, both designated National Important Cultural Properties, remained on their original sites and served as the main attractions of the new theme park. The former Alt House, also designated a National Important Cultural Property and preserved *in situ*, would join the roster of heritage buildings in 1977.

Glover Garden quickly rose shoulder to shoulder with Meiji Village as one of Japan's best-known tourist attractions, welcoming as many as two million visitors a year and infusing energy into the local economy. But there were negative consequences as well. One was the fencing off of a large section of Minamiyamate, which to date had been an ordinary, if unique, working neighborhood of Nagasaki. Another was confusion caused by the mishmash of original and relocated buildings and the subordination of historical fact to whim and decoration.

Today, visitors to Glover Garden pass what was once a tennis court on the hillside above the former Glover House and negotiate the narrow lawn in front of the former Ringer House before arriving in the garden of a stunning Western-style residence grander in size and style than the other two houses. This is the former Alt House.

To the right, the Mitsubishi Nagasaki Shipyard stretches in a tangle of docks and factories along the opposite shore of Nagasaki Harbor. In the background straight ahead, the tight-knit residential neighborhood of Ueda-machi looms on the steep hillside like seating in an amphitheater. The former Steele Academy, a two-story school building relocated from Higashiyamate in 1974, stands in the corner of the compound with its back to the harbor, the only relocated building in Glover Garden erected on the same lot as a National Important Cultural Property.

The former Alt House stands at the base of a low cliff to the left, evoking the style of a bungalow in British India, with sandstone walls and a row of Tuscan pillars marching along the front of a wide stone-paved veranda, with a protruding portico punctuated by an ornate stone fountain, and with all the nostalgic nuances of the European colonial presence in East Asia.

The hipped roof is covered in ceramic tiles, evidence of the early meeting of Japanese and European building materials and architectural designs, while vents under the veranda lead into a crawl space similar to those in traditional Japanese houses. Inside, the entrance vestibule continues in an L-shape to a wide corridor passing through the center of the building, punctuated with doors to spacious high-ceilinged rooms. A sheltered corridor leading out the rear entrance connects the main building to a brick structure with a kitchen, pantry and servants' rooms.

Yet despite the well-preserved physical condition of the building, the interior suggests that the decorators had scant information about the original position of furniture and ornaments or the function of individual rooms: desks are placed in former bedrooms, chairs have their backs to fireplaces, and walls once covered with paintings and photographs are oddly blank. Similarly, most of the pamphlets and books available on the subject of Glover Garden emphasize architectural features and gloss over stories of the buildings and the people who once lived there.

At the time of this writing, the house is hidden from view behind scaffolding, undergoing repairs to improve its resistance to earthquakes. It is hoped that when the building is reopened to the public, the refurbishments will have provided an opportunity to revamp the interior displays on the basis of systematic research and the collection of period artifacts.

The following chapters describe the history of the former Alt House at No. 14 Minamiyamate, introduce its former inhabitants and functions, and outline the events that crisscrossed there from 1859, the year that Japan awakened from a long slumber and opened its doors to international engagement, until the postwar period when Nagasaki cleared the rubble of wartime destruction and chose tourism as a step to recovery.

Brian Burke-Gaffney
Nagasaki, 2023

Chapter 1
W.J. Alt and the Pre-Meiji Years

A twelve-year-old boy named William John Alt stood on the India Docks in London, waiting to board the 730-ton full-rigged sailing vessel *Charlotte Jane*. It was early 1853, the same year that an American naval mission headed by Commodore Matthew Perry visited Japan and pried open the country's long closed doors. Daniel Alt, the boy's father and an officer in the British Army's 63rd Regiment, had recently died, leaving a widow and eight children with little money, and William had embarked on a traditional maritime career to relieve his mother's burden. The *Charlotte Jane* was already famous as one of the first four ships to carry emigrants from England to the newly founded colony of Canterbury, New Zealand.

Over the next four years, the ship zigzagged the oceans connecting Europe and New Zealand, Australia and Bermuda. William learned the rudiments of navigation under Captain Russell and used his free time to read and augment his education. While the ship anchored in Shanghai in October 1857, he met a Portuguese merchant named D. de Barros and, with the encouragement of his captain, accepted an offer of employment at an initial salary of £120 per year, with a promise that he would be able to live "like a lord and before three years be able to send home a very considerable sum of money."[1]

---

[1] William J. Alt to his mother, November 6, 1857 (W.J. Alt Letters, WA09-001a,b). Currently preserved at the Nagasaki Museum of History and Culture, the letters were donated to Nagasaki City by descendants of William J. Alt.

When the Portuguese merchant's business failed the follow-ing year, Alt took up a position in the Imperial Maritime Customs Service, an organization established in 1854 by the foreign consuls of Shanghai to collect maritime trade taxes. The new job was lucrative and gave the now eighteen-year-old William J. Alt hands-on training in the ways of international commerce. But the young Briton was restless and ambitious, anxious to make his mark on the world.

In 1858, the Tokugawa Shogunate signed the Ansei Five-Power Treaties with the United States, Britain, France, Russia and the Netherlands and opened a few Japanese ports to a new era of commercial, political and cultural interaction. The treaties guaran-teed the rights of foreigners to live and conduct business in the ports, to erect buildings on lots provided for rent in designated foreign settlements, and to enjoy the privilege of extraterritoriality (immunity from local laws). In Nagasaki, the Shogunate agreed to reclaim land from the harbor near the village of Tomachi Ōura south of the old city, as well as to install gutters, stairs and embankment walls and to prepare lots for the buildings soon to be erected by foreigners.

The contractor engaged to conduct the groundwork was Kokuminsha, a company operated by members of the Koyama family of Amakusa (in modern-day Kumamoto Prefecture) who had long experience in shipbuilding and civil engineering projects. Among the family leaders was Koyama Hidenoshin, the future builder of Ōura Catholic Church, the Glover and Alt residences and other iconic structures in the Nagasaki Foreign Settlement.[2]

Officially opened for trade on July 1, 1859, Nagasaki saw an influx of foreign merchants competing for access to the long-secluded country and its untold resources. Among the early arrivals was William J. Alt, still only nineteen years old but already experienced in the means and manners of trade through his work in Shanghai. In a letter from Nagasaki dated February 3, 1860, Alt informs his mother for the first time that he retired from the Imperial Maritime Customs Service in Shanghai and established himself as an independent commission agent in Japan:

---

[2] Kitano Norio, *Amakusa kaigai hattenshi* (History of Amakusa in Overseas Development) (Fukuoka: Ashi Shobō, 1985) Vol.1, 153-237

…having nothing to do in Shanghai and not being able to lead an idle life I took a passage in a vessel which belongs to the captain for this port and finding this a most splendid country and seeing a good opening for a persevering young fellow like myself I determined to settle here. So I returned to Shanghai and made arrangements for establishing myself here as a commission merchant, and I am now I think in a fair way of making a fortune in earnest. I received $400 for three months' salary when I was paid off from the Custom House and the captain of the vessel offered to put $1,500 more if I would give him a third share of my business which I consented to so that I started with a capital of $2,000. The captain did not charge me anything for my passage all the time I was with him on board and I received letters of introduction from the head of the house of Jardine, Matheson & Co. to their agent here and I have the promise of a good deal of business. I brought with me [a cargo of] $5,000, my commission upon which amounted to $200, which is £100 in one month. If I do the same thing every month [I] will do very well although I have been to a great deal of expense in fitting up a house and office and have to employ there a few Chinamen and several Japanese servants… I am rather young to be in my own hook on such a large scale but unless we make an attempt we do not know what we can do. My knowledge of Chinese is a great assistance to me and I am already picking up some Japanese which is far easier than Chinese. I will at my leisure send you all a big account of Japan and the Japanese but if my business increases I may rather have to employ a clerk or neglect a good deal of it as I really [have] more than I can possibly do.[3]

The first list of land renters in the Nagasaki Foreign Settlement was compiled on October 10, 1860, while the ground works were still in progress.[4] William J. Alt won the right to rent No. 7 Ōura, an ideal location at the center of the bund. Coined in British India, the word *bund* had come into common use throughout East

---

[3] William J. Alt to his mother, February 3, 1860 (Alt Letters, WA03-015a,b)

[4] George Morrison to Rutherford Alcock, October 13, 1860 (FO 262/19)

Asia and referred to the waterfront street in ports where Europeans conduced business.

Less than a year had passed since his arrival in Nagasaki, but the young Briton had already earned enough commission on import and export cargo and secured such a leading position in the foreign community that he was able to jump to the front of the queue in choosing a place for his company. He further demonstrated his business success in the summer of 1861 by hiring Scottish shipbuilder James Mitchell to build and launch the *Phantom*, Japan's first Western-style yacht.[5]

Taken in October 1860, Pierre Rossier's photograph of the proposed site of the Nagasaki Foreign Settlement was one of the first panoramic portraits taken in Japan. The huts of Tomachi Ōura village cluster in the foreground, with the mud flats at the mouth of Sagarimatsu Creek beyond. Myōgyōji, the site of Japan's first British consulate, is visible on the opposite hillside with its flagpole flying the Union Jack. Three years after this photograph was taken, Thomas Glover would build a private residence at the base of the pine tree on the crest of the hill. (National Archives, Kew, FO 46/8)

---

[5] *The Nagasaki Shipping List and Advertiser*, July 24, 1861. The newspaper article describes the launching of the yacht in detail, along with information on its style and dimensions. It is not clear what happened to the *Phantom* after Alt left Nagasaki.

The construction of buildings started as soon as the teams of Japanese laborers raked the last pile of gravel flat in the new commercial district of Ōura. The carpenters noted the specifications submitted by foreign renters regarding the size and shape of doors, windows and floors and the installment of chimneys and other European fixtures. But they naturally implemented indigenous building techniques and relied on the materials they had been using for generations in traditional buildings. The result was an unprecedented coalescence of Japanese and European architectural designs.

Records are scarce, but it is likely that William J. Alt engaged the Koyama family—who had supervised the reclamation of land from the harbor—to construct the Alt & Co. office building at No. 7 Ōura. One of the first and most prominent buildings in the commercial district, the two-story Western-style wooden structure featured a high pyramidal roof covered in ceramic tiles, surrounding verandas on both floors, and brick chimneys sprouting from coal-burning fireplaces. The building was ready for occupancy by April 15, 1862, when the British and American consuls issued orders for all foreign residents to move out of the Japanese town and into the confines of the foreign settlement.

Ōura Bund seen from Minamiyamate circa 1865. Alt & Co. occupied the large two-story building built at the center of the waterfront bund. Dejima and the city streets of Nagasaki are visible in the background. (Private collection)

Alt & Co. surged ahead on the wave of business in Nagasaki. The windfall from trade allowed Alt to acquire further properties in the foreign settlement and to expand his range of activities. In response to the demand abroad for Japanese tea, he established tea-firing factories in the rear quarter behind his office and hired hundreds of Japanese and Chinese workers to dry the raw tea using pans installed on long fireplaces and to pack the finished product for shipment. The factories operated day and night to meet the orders pouring in. Tea quickly replaced seafood and vegetable wax as the principal export item from Nagasaki, exerting a huge impact on the local economy and providing work for a long line of local merchants and laborers stretching into the hinterland.

William J. Alt also played a leading role in foreign settlement society, serving as a representative of the municipal council and heading committees to discuss everything from the construction of a Protestant church to the opening of a foreign cemetery and the establishment of a fire brigade.

The Development of Minamiyamate

The area granted by the Tokugawa Shogunate for the Nagasaki Foreign Settlement did not originally include the hillside districts that would later develop into leafy residential neighborhoods scattered with Western-style houses. The demarcation of lots for rental to foreigners started from the commercial districts of Ōura and Sagarimatsu facing the harbor and creek. Only later, and reluctantly, did Japanese authorities bend to requests from foreign consuls for residential lots on the Higashiyamate hillside (Ōura Hill). The "hill lots" had a prototype in British hill stations in India and the terraced heights in Canton and Hong Kong where foreigners could enjoy not only panoramic vistas and cool breezes but also an escape from the clash of cultures in the steamy cities below.

Minamiyamate was the last bone of contention in the land concessions to foreigners. In a letter dated April 13, 1861, British Consul George S. Morrison informed his superior Rutherford Alcock that, because Japanese authorities continued to oppose the development of the hillside south of the Buddhist temple Myōgyōji (site of the Nagasaki British Consulate at the time), he had conferred with the governor and submitted his personal request, pointing out that space was needed for the health and comfort of residents and that the existing settlement was too cramped to accommodate the rapidly growing foreign population. It was the first time for the consul to sit at the same table with the governor, rather than on opposite sides of the room as in the past. When the governor gave the stock answer that he would have to consult with the Shogunate in Edo, Morrison pressed for an immediate decision, cleverly suggesting that the rental of Minamiyamate lots could be adopted as a *temporary* measure.[6]

Up to that point, the mostly deforested Minamiyamate hillside had been the site of fields where farmers raised oranges, loquats and vegetables for the Nagasaki market. The only road was the old horse path extending from Myōgyōji along the spine of Nagasaki Peninsula to Cape Nomo. The hillside overlooked the long inlet of Nagasaki Harbor and the backdrop of green-clad mountains, from the congested streets of Nagasaki on the right to the harbor entrance dotted with small islands in the distance on the left.

By September 1861, the governor had agreed to extend the borders of the foreign settlement as far as the foot of the hill below Kotohira Shinto Shrine, an area of about seventeen hectares to be divided into thirty-five lots numbered according to their proximity to Myōgyōji. A group of renters stepped forward that month to claim rights to the first available lots, that is, Nos. 1 to 11. A young native of Aberdeenshire, Scotland named Thomas B. Glover acquired the lease to No. 3 Minamiyamate, one of the most scenic lots on the hillside and the site of a landmark pine tree. Glover had arrived in Nagasaki in September 1859, a few steps ahead of William J. Alt, to serve in the local office of Jardine, Matheson & Co.

William J. Alt, meanwhile, snapped up No. 9 Minamiyamate, a lot on the crest of a rocky outcrop at the foot of the hillside. The census conducted by Japanese authorities in October 1862[7] indicates the presence of a building on the site, probably the bungalow to which Alt would refer in correspondence the following year. Coined in India from the Hindi word *bangala* (Bengali), bungalow was used

---

[6] George S. Morrison to Rutherford Alcock, April 13, 1861 (FO 262/29)
[7] Nagasaki Prefecture ed., *Nagasaki kyoryūchi gaikokujin meibo I* (List of Foreign Residents of the Nagasaki Foreign Settlement, Vol.1), (Nagasaki Prefectural Library, 2004), 12

to denote the single-story houses with wide verandas common in that region. It had followed the path of British influence from India to Japan via the ports of Malaysia and China, coming to refer to the opulent houses built on sunlit hillsides above the treaty ports where Britons and other foreigners conducted business. The house built by William J. Alt at No. 9 Minamiyamate would remain intact until being demolished after World War II and replaced with a dormitory for foreign engineers visiting the Mitsubishi Nagasaki Shipyard.[8]

The Glover House at No. 3 Minamiyamate circa 1866, with the landmark pine tree looming behind. The greenhouse built by Glover is visible in the foreground, one of the earliest examples of a European-style greenhouse in Japan. The stone bungalow of William J. Alt was under construction at the time of this photograph. The people on the right have not been identified. (Courtesy of David Carmichael)

---

[8] The former house at No. 9 Minamiyamate is also known as the place where Thomas B. Glover's British-Japanese son Kuraba Tomisaburō committed suicide a few days after the end of World War II.

Thomas B. Glover's house at No. 3 Minamiyamate remains today as the oldest Western-style building in Japan and a UNESCO World Heritage Site. Completed in 1863 (the year after the young Aberdonian established Glover & Co.), the single-story wooden bungalow features semicircular protrusions with hipped roofs, stone-paved porches, timber columns, arched doorways and latticed ceilings. The roof is built in traditional Japanese style with ceramic tiles laid over a layer of clay. The outer walls, although rendered in Western fashion, conceal *tsuchikabe* (earthen walls) reinforced with rope, bamboo strips and seaweed. Inside, the house presents a typical Western-style appearance: living and dining rooms at the front and bedrooms in the rear, with hardwood floors and English-style coal-burning fireplaces and stone mantels. Although no exact record exists, the builder was probably Koyama Hidenoshin.[9]

Pistols under their Bedcovers

Thomas B. Glover may have celebrated the completion of his house, but the mood among foreign residents was anything but jovial. A British merchant from Shanghai had been killed the previous autumn by retainers of the Satsuma Domain when his horse interfered with the daimyo's procession on a narrow road near Yokohama. Tensions escalated when the Satsuma Domain refused to accept responsibility for the incident, sending ripples of fear through the foreign community of Nagasaki as the closest treaty port to Kagoshima. British residents called an emergency meeting on May 13, 1863 to decide whether or not to abandon the settlement.[10] William J. Alt and Thomas B. Glover chose to stay, stowing their valuables on British ships anchored in Nagasaki Harbor, gathering for mutual protection in the Alt & Co. office at night, and sleeping with pistols under their bedcovers. The suspense rose to a climax in August 1863 when the

---

[9] The circumstances of the project remain unclear, including the names of the architect and builder. The only source of information is a plaque discovered in the rafters of the house during refurbishments conducted in 1966. Rendered in *sumi* ink on a slab of wood, the inscription gives the date 1863 and the signatures of Kumaichi and Mokichi, presumably two of the carpenters working under Koyama Hidenoshin.

[10] FO 262/60/28-9

British bombarded the city of Kagoshima. Duly impressed, Shimazu Hisamitsu, father of the daimyo and *de facto* leader of the Satsuma Domain, acknowledged the importance of promoting trade and industry in cooperation with the countries of the West.

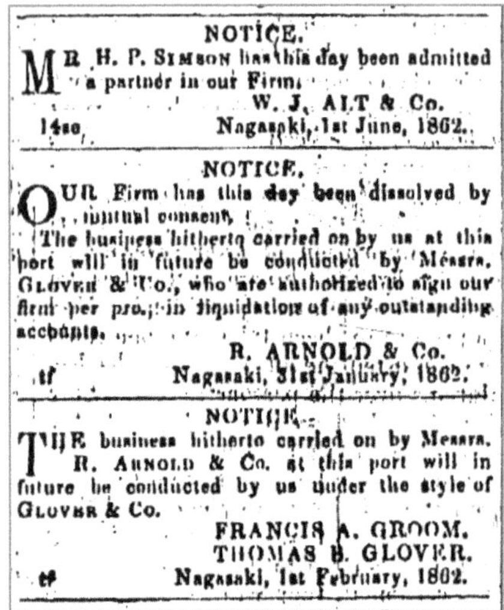

NOTICE.

MR. H. P. SIMSON has this day been admitted a partner in our Firm.

W. J. ALT & Co.

14so, Nagasaki, 1st June, 1862.

NOTICE.

OUR Firm has this day been dissolved by mutual consent.

The business hitherto carried on by us at this port will in future be conducted by Messrs. Glover & Co., who are authorized to sign our firm per pro., in liquidation of any outstanding accounts.

R. ARNOLD & Co.

Nagasaki, 31st January, 1862.

NOTICE.

THE business hitherto carried on by Messrs. R. Arnold & Co. at this port will in future be conducted by us under the style of Glover & Co.

FRANCIS A. GROOM.
THOMAS B. GLOVER.

Nagasaki, 1st February, 1862.

William J. Alt reported the appointment of Henry P. Simson as his partner in the Yokohama newspaper *The Japan Herald.* Simson would soon acquire the lease to the No. 14 Minamiyamate lot and begin the construction of a stone bungalow. in the same newspaper, Thomas B. Glover announced the purchase of the business run formerly by Briton Robert Arnold and the launching of Glover & Co. (Right) W.J. Alt circa 1866. (Courtesy of David Carmichael)

One of the outcomes of the reconciliation between Britain and the Satsuma Domain was a jump in the demand for second-hand steamships, expensive items but essential means for the domains of southwestern Japan to promote trade and transportation. In a long letter dated October 15, 1863, William J. Alt informs his mother that he traveled from Nagasaki to Hong Kong to fetch a steamship ordered by the Nagasaki *bugyō* (magistrate, called the "governor" by foreign residents). About the steamship, he says:

She is a very nice vessel indeed and I am having her docked and thoroughly cleaned and painted up inside and putting carpets in the cabins and also some pictures etc. so as to take the eye of the old Governor of Nagasaki when he sees her. I am sure that he will be pleased with her when he sees her, and if he only takes her as promised why as I said before we shall make a small pot of money out of her which will be very good after such an unfortunate year as this has been. And it will enable me to go home at the beginning of the year much happier than I could otherwise.[11]

Alt indeed managed to make the trip to England in early 1864, leaving the affairs of Alt & Co. in the hands of Henry P. Simson, his business partner since June 1862. The voyage was an auspicious one. Along the way, the young Briton met and fell in love with his future wife Elisabeth Christiana Earl. Elisabeth was the only child of George Windsor Earl, a celebrated geographer, ethnologist, colonial administrator, and the author of several groundbreaking books. He is attributed with coining the term "Indu-nesian," later popularized and adopted as the name of Indonesia.[12]

On the return voyage from England, Alt traveled to Australia to reunite with Elisabeth, and the couple wed at Holy Trinity Church, Adelaide on September 15. He was twenty-four years old; Elisabeth was seventeen. The newlyweds returned to Nagasaki in November 1864 and took up residence in the bungalow at No. 9 Minamiyamate. George Windsor Earl died the following year in Penang, and Elisabeth's mother Clara sailed to Nagasaki and joined the Alt family at the behest of her daughter and son-in-law.

Elisabeth Alt later remembered Nagasaki as "the first part of Japan where I lived for four years" and "certainly a vision of beauty. I cannot think of a more beautiful place." However, she also told her children that she had wept upon discovering that "there was no fresh milk ever to be had" in Japan. She gave birth to her first daughter, Mabel, on July 2, 1865.

---

[11] William J. Alt to his mother, October 15, 1863 (Alt Letters, WA05-010_01a)

[12] Ranald Noel-Paton, *An Eastern Calling: George Windsor Earl and a Vision of Empire* (Ashgrove Publishing, 2018), 185

Elisabeth Alt (nee Earl) in Nagasaki circa 1866. (Right) Mabel Alt with her amah and a Japanese maid, apparently taken on the veranda at No. 9 Minamiyamate. (Courtesy of David Carmichael)

As the wave of development of the Minamiyamate hillside and construction of buildings extended southward in 1863, William J. Alt's business partner Henry P. Simson obtained the perpetual lease to No. 14 Minamiyamate, a spacious lot on a level slightly higher than the Glover house and further south on the hillside. A native of Wigtown, Scotland and former resident of Singapore, Simson was the sole renter and clearly intended to erect a house for his own use on the property. Among the materials in the Koyama family archive is an architect's floor plan executed in ink on Kent paper with a watermark reading "C. Ansell 1863."[13] No other information is available regarding the architect, but it seems likely that Simson commissioned the floor plan as part of his preparations for the house at No. 14 Minamiyamate.

---

[13] The paper was undoubtedly made by C. Ansell, a company producing watermarked paper in Carshalton, Surrey.

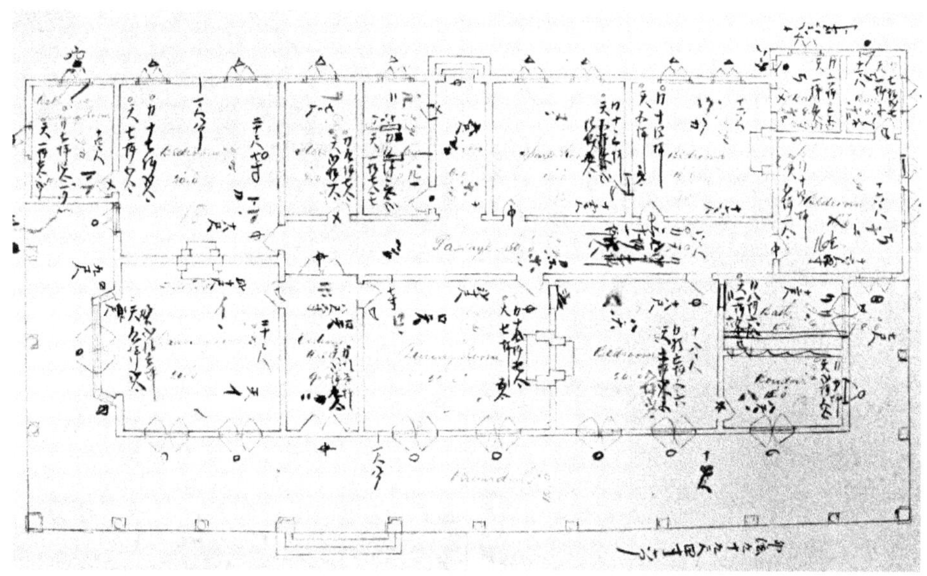

Floor plan of the house at No. 14 Minamiyamate. The carpenters jotted notes in Japanese over the original document executed in ink by an unknown British architect. The document sheds light on the early meeting of European and Japanese architecture. (Nagasaki City Museum of History and Folklore)

In a letter to the Nagasaki Magistrate in December the same year, British Consul Francis G. Myburgh relayed Simson's request for an extension of the Minamiyamate lot to avoid a large mass of rock obstructing the construction of the house:

> Although the request was a reasonable one, still the Land Officer refuses it. Mr. Simson has gone to great expense to prepare a proper platform, whereon to build a house, and this will be quite useless to him, on account of the quantity of stone in the way, unless a small space be added to make up for the loss of the space occupied by the stone. It is for this small addition that I now make application to you on Mr. Simson's behalf, and I hope you will be good enough to accede to it.[14]

---

[14] Francis G. Myburgh to Hattori Nagatonokami, December 29, 1863, *Raikan* [Official correspondence from foreign nationals to the Nagasaki Prefecture government] 1863, (Nagasaki Museum of History and Culture).

Simson may have spent more than a year trying to solve the problem of the offending rock because only in May 1865 do the Japanese census surveys mention a building under construction.[15] In fact, he seems to have turned the project over entirely to William J. Alt. British Consulate records show that from April 1, 1865, he was no longer the sole renter but shared the lease with Alt.[16] Interestingly, Simson left Nagasaki for Yokohama the same month and stayed there until his death on September 4, 1865 at the age of thirty-three. Aside from the report on his burial in the Yokohama Foreign Cemetery[17] and a few other snippets of information in the above documents, the story of his life and work has faded into obscurity.

Japan's First Protestant Church

The first building erected by Koyama Hidenoshin on the hillsides of the Nagasaki Foreign Settlement was the Protestant church at No. 11 Higashiyamate, a small wooden building constructed under contract from British residents and completed in 1862. After finishing the Glover House at No. 3 Minamiyamate the following year, Koyama accepted a request from missionaries of the Société des Mission Etrangères de Paris (Paris Foreign Missions Society) to construct a Catholic church at No. 1A Minamiyamate. The new church was similar to the Protestant church, but the features demanded by the French priests—such as altar, choir loft, lectern, confessionals and rib-vault ceilings—provided Koyama with a far more sophisticated introduction to the traditions of European cathedral architecture, a style with few parallels in his Japanese repertory. Only a few weeks after the dedication in February 1865, a group of peasants from the village of Urakami north of Nagasaki visited the church and revealed their faith to the French priest Bernard Petitjean, marking the sensational discovery of the hidden Japanese Christians after a more than two-century long hibernation.

---

[15] Nagasaki Prefecture ed., *Nagasaki kyoryūchi gaikokujin meibo I* (List of Foreign Residents of the Nagasaki Foreign Settlement, Vol.1), (Nagasaki Prefectural Library, 2004), 102

[16] FO 796/203/141

[17] *The Japan Herald*, September 9, 1865. The cause of death is not mentioned.

The foreign residents of Nagasaki were allowed an outing to Nezumijima (Rat Island) in the spring of 1865. William J. Alt is sitting (left, center) with a small dog in his lap. Elisabeth (white dress) is behind him. Thomas Glover is sitting front center with legs extended and his hat on his foot. (Nagasaki University Library)

That spring, Koyama Hidenoshin brought all his experience and knowledge to a challenging new project: the construction of a house at No. 14 Minamiyamate, a 2,000 *tsubo* (1.63 acre) lot and one of the largest and most scenically situated pieces of land in the Nagasaki Foreign Settlement. Koyama took the floor plan commissioned by Henry P. Simson and superimposed room names and dimensions in Japanese on the original pen script, providing evidence of one of the earliest encounters of European and traditional Japanese architecture. William J. Alt undoubtedly consulted with Koyama about the details of the building and provided all the necessary funds. According to the consular record, Alt obtained sole rights to the property on January 4, 1866. In the census conducted by Japanese authorities in May the same year, he is shown as residing for the first time at No. 14 Minamiyamate with his wife, daughter and mother-in-law.

The magnificent wood and stone bungalow was a remarkable achievement given its unprecedented architectural style. The versatile master carpenter probably balked at the idea of a house with stone walls in the humid climate of Nagasaki, but he responded to Alt's requests and piled sandstone plates over exterior walls, producing the earliest example of colonial-style stone-and-timber architecture in Japan. Under the stone, however, were traditional *tsuchikabe* (earthen walls) fashioned with thick mud mixed with straw and seaweed and pressed into a lattice of rope and bamboo strips. Koyama paved the wide veranda and erected a row of supporting columns, all fashioned from the same pink sandstone quarried on the island of Amakusa and carried to Nagasaki by ship, then hauled up the hillside by teams of laborers.

The house at No. 14 Minamiyamate seen from the hillside circa 1868. The Glover House and pine tree are visible on the left. A person can be seen pushing a roller in the garden in the foreground, evidence of one of the first grass lawns in Japan. The Italianate fountain in front of the portico was also part of the original structure. (Courtesy of Sam Hunt)

Rectangular in shape, the main building had a floor space of about 500 square meters, with rooms arranged along a wide L-shaped corridor running through the interior. All the windows, doorways and fireplaces were executed in European fashion, but the hipped roof was covered in ceramic tiles identical to those used in Japanese houses. Another notable feature was a gabled portico protruding from the main door and, in front of it, an Italianate fountain, probably the first of its kind in Japan.

The photograph of the house taken soon after completion proves that the fountain was part of the original construction. The photograph also shows a worker pushing a heavy roller used to flatten lawns, evidence that Alt introduced British garden styles to Japan along with his unique stone bungalow. Created in northern Europe to simulate pastureland in the garden context, the grass lawn was already a standard fixture in British country estates and large urban homes by the time Alt deemed it appropriate for his grand residence in Nagasaki. As a place for cool storage, Koyama also dug a nine-meter-deep cave out of the rocky cliff at the back of the property, a novelty that remains intact to this day.

A Forest of Posts

Some foreign observers doubted the architectural integrity and durability of the buildings appearing in the foreign settlements, European in style but erected by Japanese carpenters using traditional methods and materials. One was R.H. Brunton, a British engineer invited to Japan to supervise public works such as the construction of the Iojima lighthouse in Nagasaki. In a paper read before the Asiatic Society of Japan in January 1875, Brunton described the typical wooden Japanese house, built on a low stone foundation with the uprights forming the walls placed from two to three feet apart "so that when they are still uncovered they appear like a forest of posts."[18] He also pointed out that, "very few houses in the foreign settlements are built after a more secure and substantial style, and in Japanese hands it has, if anything, become worse." Continues Brunton:

---

[18] *The Japan Weekly Mail*, January 23, 1875

When foreigners first arrived in this country they may have had reasons for adopting this method of construction. 1st.—It is somewhat similar to the Japanese method and those who commenced building might have been glad to adopt it on that account as the work would be more or less familiar to the only workmen who were available at the time. 2nd.—It has the advantage of only requiring the very cheapest and most easily procured materials, and so is well suited for temporary purposes or for hasty erection. 3rd.—It is supposed by some persons to be the best construction to resist earthquakes on account of its elasticity and on account of the wooden framework preventing the outside lining of stones or other covering from being precipitated inwards on the occasion of a shock... For merely temporary buildings it may still be, on account of its cheapness, the best, but if the construction is to have any pretensions to be a lasting erection, or one which has to afford effectual protection from outside disturbances, I have no hesitation In saying that the system Is the most uneconomical. From the fragile nature of the materials forming the outside casing, whether these are stone flags, tiles or merely plaster, the walls are in want of constant repair, and are never water or airtight.

If R.H. Brunton were alive today, he might be surprised to see how well some of the buildings on the Minamiyamate hillside, including the house erected by Koyama Hidenoshin for William J. Alt, have withstood the trials of time, weather and "outside disturbances."

Friendships with the Rulers of Japan

William J. Alt paid the huge cost of his new house from the rich proceeds of business dealings, which by 1868 had come to include several shipping and insurance agencies in addition to the traditional exchange of tea and other Japanese products for fabrics, aromatic wood and the various exotic commodities demanded by his customers. The import of second-hand ships also continued to provide lucrative profits. Elisabeth Alt describes her husband's activities as follows in her memoir:

I know my husband, while carrying on his business in those early days, frequently went as a guest to the chief towns and country seats of the Princes [i.e. daimyo] with whom he was friendly… He enjoyed some enchanting experiences which I am sorry he never set down for the benefit of others—of journeys up mountains to meet a great Prince, where he was carried in a litter or 'chair' along mountain paths where he hung over precipices that did not bear looking over. He was always very courteously received, and made great friendships with the men who were afterwards among the rulers of Japan—the new Japan that was even then making its way steadily to the front of the nations.[19]

Iwasaki Yatarō (1835-1885)

One of William J. Alt's closest collaborators was Iwasaki Yatarō, a young samurai of the Tosa Domain (present-day Kōchi Prefecture) who came to Nagasaki to negotiate the sale of products from his home province. Alt appears frequently in Iwasaki's diaries, including mention of his assistance in clearing the name of Tosa samurai after the murder of two British sailors in Nagasaki in the summer of 1867, a tragedy that accelerated the collapse of the old order in Japan. The same year, Alt and Iwasaki departed Nagasaki for a ride on horseback. When they were stopped at a checkpoint outside the city, Alt suggested that they turn back because foreigners were not allowed to go beyond the boundaries defined by treaty. But

---

[19] Phillis Alt, *An Extract from the Memoirs of Elisabeth Christina Alt, Nee Earl, Who Lived in Nagasaki from 1864-68, Together with an Abridged Biographical Sketch of Her Parents* (1985.)

Iwasaki convinced the sentry to let them pass by cleverly warning that a refusal might incite an international conflict.[20] The anecdote reveals, not only the friendship between the two men, but also the obstacles faced by foreigners when trying to visit the interior.

In 1868, Iwasaki Yatarō moved his center of activity to Osaka, where he founded an enterprise called Tsukumo Shōkai and launched a steamship service on the Seto Inland Sea. The company would undergo a number of name changes before emerging as the Mitsubishi Mail Steamship Co., a leading presence in Japan's burgeoning domestic and international shipping industry and the predecessor of the modern-day Mitsubishi conglomerate.

William J. Alt as a young man in Japan.
(Minato City Local History Museum)

---

[20] *Iwasaki Yatarō Den* (The Biography of Iwasaki Yatarō, Vol. 1), 381

"The Winning Crew" is captured in a photograph taken after the Nagasaki Regatta in May 1866. The five are (left to right) Frederick Ringer, W.O. Forster, William J. Alt, John C. Smith and Robert Hughes. Ringer, Smith and Hughes were employees of Glover & Co. Alt, Ringer and Smith would all be intimately associated with the house at No. 14 Minamiyamate. (Courtesy of David Carmichael)

The Alt family continued to live happily in the grand house at No. 14 Minamiyamate and to play a vital role in both the social life of the Nagasaki Foreign Settlement and international business in the Japanese port. By the summer of 1868, the family included William and Elisabeth, Elisabeth's mother Clara Earl, daughters Mabel, Ethel (born on December 20, 1866) and Kathleen (born on August 9, 1868), as well as an amah and several servants. Although her name does not appear in any records of the time, the amah was probably the woman holding Mabel on her knee in the photograph (p. 26) taken in 1866, a foreigner whose facial features and dress suggest Southeast Asian or Aboriginal Australian roots.

Despite the enormous time and expense invested in the opulent house at No. 14 Minamiyamate and his many business successes in Nagasaki, William J. Alt decided to leave for the greener pastures of Osaka in 1868, one motivating factor probably being the establishment of Tsukumo Shōkai by his friend Iwasaki Yatarō the same year. Alt entrusted his operations in Nagasaki to leading employees and moved to the "Venice of the East," where he opened a branch office in the newly established Kawaguchi Foreign Settlement. Elisabeth and her three daughters, accompanied by the children's amah, boarded the steamship *Osaka* in November 1868 and sailed out of Nagasaki Harbor never to return.[21]

A New Life in Osaka, Yokohama and England

William J. Alt would remain in Osaka for eighteen months—and his business would flourish as expected—but Elisabeth apparently found her living conditions far less favorable than those of the lavish Western-style house she had left behind in Nagasaki:

> The stay at Osaka was the most unpleasant part of my seven years in the country. It was a city built on many rivers and canals and had seventy bridges, it was said. We lived in a Japanese house—a fair-sized one, but the size of the rooms, the low ceilings, the paper windows were very unsuitable to Europeans. Especially as it was a very cold climate. Everything that could be done to make the house comfortable was done. In our sitting

---

21 *The Nagasaki Times*, November 14, 1868

room we had glass windows put in instead of paper and a brick fireplace was built, mostly by my husband's own hands as the people understood neither chimneys nor bricks. But the other rooms were very cold and very trying to our three little children.

Elisabeth goes on to provide a vivid description of the method of payment in business dealings and the difficulty of depositing money securely in a foreign bank, a situation that undoubtedly continued from the years in Nagasaki:

My husband had large dealings with the Government and the different princes who were more or less independent in those days. Large contracts were entered into and it happened that unexpectedly, to fulfil one of these contracts, the prince in question sent down from his province the sum of money to pay for it in solid silver—in the usual coin of the country, <u>icheboos</u> [silver *ichibu*], which were oblong and easily packed, worth about eighteenpence of our money (at least it was in those days). I think my husband did not expect so prompt a payment, nor did he expect it in that form. However, the money was there and had to be received. Osaka was rather a lawless place with many rogues about and the knowledge that these people might be aware of what was happening made it necessary to take precautions against any attack from some of the cleverest criminals in the country. The boxes of silver icheboos were carried in by two coolies at a time and were packed into the entrance well-like recess, which was gradually filled up until it was level with the floor of the rest of the house. It was night time when this was doing and it was a picturesque sight by the dim lantern light seeing these half-naked men (for the Japanese coolie or labourer does not spend much on clothes, preferring a good deal of tattoo to take its place; the illusion of clothes is good and must be convenient in summer). This scene must have been in warm weather for I remember the perspiring coolies. When all had been carried in and the gates were shut and the wooden shutters carefully closed, the native staff of the business establishment collected their sleeping mats and quilts which were spread on the top of the boxes of coins, and there they slept the night while the Englishmen took as much rest as they could in their anxiety.

In 1870, William J. Alt moved his place of business and residence to the Yokohama Foreign Settlement, which provided familiar living conditions among fellow British expatriates as well as more convenient methods of business. But even in the latter port, he and his wife Elisabeth probably thought back wistfully about the house at No. 14 Minamiyamate and the months spent in the lap of Western-style comforts and natural beauty in Nagasaki.

The following year, suffering from chronic bronchial disease, Alt finally decided to leave his business activities in the hands of colleagues and return to England. He had been in Japan for little more than a decade, but the now thirty-one-year-old Briton had amassed such a fortune that he was able to enjoy the rest of his life in ease amid the trappings of nobility. He had also gathered a huge collection of prized Japanese art works, many of them gifts from the provincial daimyo with whom he had engaged in business over the years.

In the addendum to her mother's memoir, Phillis Alt describes the art collection as follows:

> The beautiful collection of Japanese objets d'art, many given to William Alt by his Prince friends, was exhibited in London after his return to England. They included kakimonos, bronzes, nitsuke statuettes, precious porcelain (Satsuma and other ware, all of the loveliest colouring) and cloisonné. Very charming too was a series of tiny paintings illustrating a journey to the sacred Mountain Fujiyama, and a small shrine holding wonderfully carved deities. Sadly, this large collection could not be kept intact as the family moved to smaller houses. They were gradually sold over the years and some given to museums.

The family, including a son born in Yokohama and named George Earl after his maternal grandfather, took up residence in a palatial house in Woburn Park, Surrey surrounded by fields and woods.[22] Three more daughters joined the brood, bringing the total to seven, but financial difficulties forced William to sell the house in 1877 and move into the more modest accommodations in London where his second son and eighth child Brian Lancelot was born.

---

22 The house remains to this day as part of St. George's College, Weybridge (www.stgeorgesweybridge.com/who-are-we/our-history)

With regard to William J. Alt's sunset years in England and the fate of his two sons, Phillis Alt continues as follows in her addendum to her mother's memoir:

William Alt was a conservative in politics, a keen Imperialist and an ardent believer in the need for Home Defence. For this reason, he worked untiringly for the Volunteers, become Colonel of the 22nd London Middlesex Regiment. In later life he was awarded the Companion of the Order of the Bath [an honor second only to knighthood]. Brian, the younger son, became a Volunteer also, and left Oxford University to join a regiment raised when things were not going well during the South African War, and was killed at Diamond Hill in 1900 aged 23. Their elder son, George, was killed in the Great War in 1916.

The Alt family after their return to England. (Top row, left to right) Kathleen, Elisabeth, Ethyl (Madge), George, William J. Alt. (Seated, left to right) Clara Earl (Elisabeth's mother who joined the family in Nagasaki after her husband's death), Mabel, Anne (Nancy). (Bottom, left to right) Brian, Pleasance, Phillis. (Courtesy of Ranald Noel-Paton)

In 1898, William J. Alt purchased a villa in Rapallo, a seaside town in the province of Genoa, northern Italy frequented in the winter by wealthy Britons including Elisabeth's maternal uncle Major General Herbert Siborne. Every year until his death in 1908 at the age of sixty-eight, Alt and his family escaped from the cold rainy weather of London and relaxed on the sunny hillside of Rapallo, gazing at the blue waters of Tigullio Gulf and perhaps recalling the house at No. 14 Minamiyamate and the verdant hillside overlooking Nagasaki Harbor.

William J. Alt in later life (from the family letters)

Chapter 2
Henry J. Hunt and Family

When William J. Alt left Nagasaki in late 1868, the foreign settlement he had helped to establish was complete both physically and socially, released from the political turmoil of the past decade and ready to engage in a new era of trade and cultural exchange. The results of surveys conducted by Japanese authorities show that the foreign population of the city had grown from 397 in 1865 to 574 in late 1868, including 375 Chinese, eighty-one British, thirty-nine American, thirty Dutch, fifteen French, twenty German, eight Portuguese and six Swedish residents.[23]

The commercial districts of Ōura and Sagarimatsu and hillside residential neighborhoods of Higashiyamate and Minami-yamate were now dotted with Western-style buildings and inhabited by a growing number of foreign women and children. A Dutch consulate had replaced the former Dutch Factory on Dejima, and the island, incorporated into the foreign settlement in 1866, was now home to a number of businesses run by Dutch, German and French residents. The year 1868 also saw the abolition of the old Chinese Quarter and the absorption of the artificial island of Shinchi, formerly the site of warehouses for imported cargo, into the foreign settlement.

In the commercial districts, Glover & Co., Alt & Co. and other leading firms jostled for access to the waterfront, while a troop of smaller business establishments like Holme, Ringer & Co., Rainbow, Lewis & Co. and Maltby & Co. put out signs on the narrow streets of the rear quarter. A variety of shops and services had appeared to meet the needs of the foreign community, including a butcher's shop,

<hr>

[23] Nagasaki City Chronology, 101, 106

blacksmith's foundry and Western-style accommodations like the Belle Vue Hotel and Oriental Hotel.

Another, controversial, face of the Nagasaki Foreign Settlement was the underworld of *grog shops* catering to the crews of foreign warships and earning a reputation for drunkenness and illicit prostitution. The son of one Jewish tavern owner remembered the contrast between the neighborhood around Sagarimatsu Creek where the drinking establishments clustered and the hillside residential districts populated by wealthy British merchants and American missionaries:

> They held us up in high disgust, flaunted us contemptuously and regarded us with scorn. Every day we kids had to be on our toes. Not accepted by the better class nations, looked down upon by our own white neighbors, we were outcasts... Injustice I was cognizant of. Envy no! not a bit because of the luxurious life led by the elite neighbors who sent their children to private schools. I watched their swimming pools, their lawn parties, their beautiful garden settings and activities of their yacht and tennis club functions, etc.[24]

Despite its underdog status, the area around Sagarimatsu Creek remained the most densely populated and commercially active section of the Nagasaki Foreign Settlement, teeming with taverns, low-class hotels and shops run by blacksmiths, antique dealers and tailors. Residents and travelers rubbed shoulders on the waterfront and backstreets, coming and going with every foreign ship dropping anchor in Nagasaki Harbor. Meanwhile, the leafy hillside neighborhoods of Minamiyamate and Higashiyamate, studded with gracious Western-style houses and gardens, continued to serve as exclusive enclaves for wealthy European and American families. For a small port town separated from the centers of Japanese political power, Nagasaki also had a remarkably large number of consular representations and foreign banks.

---

[24] From a letter written by Arthur Goldenberg and quoted in: Lane R. Earns, "Life at the Bottom of the Hill: A Jewish-Japanese Family in the Nagasaki Foreign Settlement," *Crossroads: A Journal of Nagasaki History and Culture*, No. 2, Summer 1994, 82

(Above) The Ōura commercial district circa 1870. The Glover House is visible top left. (Below) The Minamiyamate district looking north toward the city of Nagasaki. No. 14 Minamiyamate is the building second from right. (Courtesy of Glover Garden)

However, Nagasaki's prominent role in the foreign trade waned after the collapse of the Tokugawa regime in 1868, when the opening of new foreign settlements in Kobe and Osaka and the rapid development of the Yokohama Foreign Settlement cut into the city's fortunes. Yokohama and Kobe were even eclipsing Nagasaki in the tea trade, particularly the export of tea to North America. The two ports enjoyed proximity to the huge tea-producing districts of Shizuoka and Uji, respectively. Moreover, instead of shipping through Nagasaki, many tea producers in Kyūshū were sending their product directly to the larger ports. Alt & Co., Glover & Co. and other foreign enterprises dealing in tea continued to face stiff competition from Chinese merchants, who outnumbered other nationalities in the foreign settlement. Thomas B. Glover declared bankruptcy in the summer of 1870, delivering yet another blow to the Nagasaki economy. Great changes were also in store for Alt & Co. and its two leading employees in Nagasaki, Henry J. Hunt and Frederick Hellyer.

Henry J. Hunt Arrives in Nagasaki

A native of Bristol, Gloucestershire, Henry Joseph Hunt left England in 1864 and traveled to China looking for a niche in the business world of the treaty ports. He visited Nagasaki for the first time in August 1867, just when the brutal murder of two British sailors on a backstreet in the Japanese town was monopolizing conversations on both sides of the language barrier. The pair, twenty-three-year-old Robert Foad and John Hutchings, had come ashore with their shipmates and proceeded to the Maruyama entertainment quarter, where they drank themselves into a stupor. Their friends had left them on the doorstep of a Japanese house to sleep it off, but when they returned they found the two men lying dead in a pool of blood and displaying the typical gashes left by swords. Hearing that a ship of the Tosa Domain had left Nagasaki Harbor the night of the murders, British Consul Marcus Flowers pointed a blaming finger at the Kaientai, a group of Tosa samurai working in Nagasaki. To prove their innocence, the Tosa samurai, with the help of Iwasaki Yatarō and William J. Alt, launched an investigation and later proved that the crime had been perpetrated by samurai of the Chikuzen (Fukuoka) Domain who had already taken responsibility by committing *seppuku* (ritual disembowelment).

Despite the apprehensions rippling through the foreign community of Nagasaki in the wake of the murders, Henry J. Hunt made daily excursions into the city and environs, observing everything from hillside graveyards to songs and dances by geisha in Maruyama. A few days after his arrival, he met an employee of Alt & Co. and accepted an invitation to go out rowing in the harbor and later to dine in the office at No. 7 Ōura.

During his three-week stay in Nagasaki, Hunt established such a relationship of trust with William J. Alt that the latter would later invite him back to Nagasaki and ask him to assume management of the Nagasaki office of Alt & Co. Hunt recalled the circumstances as follows in his diary:

> Nagasaki. Arrived here 10th August 1868, having been engaged by Mr. Lindau to take charge of Alt & Co's business here. Alt was going to Hiogo-Osaka and Lindau was going home for a trip. I took Ryley's berth as he joined Diers, Hughes soon after my arrival. I was to get £500 per annum for 3 years per agreement but it was stated that I should probably get an advance after first year. Alt left 20th Oct/68 and Lindau went home per 16th Oct Mail, so I have been in charge nearly 11 months. When I came the firm consisted of Alt and Lindau partners; Ryley general man and tea, Milne, Bookkeeper; Schöttler, just joined, Gillingham cashier etc., Hellyer Shipping and Insurance man and tea. Ryley was going to leave and Milne went with Alt to Osaka, so I was left with Schöttler as bookkeeper and Hellyer and Gillingham.[25]

Richard Lindau had been working for Walsh & Co. in Nagasaki before joining William J. Alt as a partner. In his diary entry for January 1, 1871, Hunt reports that he traveled to Yokohama to meet William J. Alt and discuss terms for Alt's retirement and the liquidation of the company. In early January, Alt and Lindau reported their withdrawal from business in the English-language press.[26] The company branch

---

[25] Transcript of the diary of Henry Joseph Hunt covering the period from 1864 to 1875 (courtesy of Sam Hunt)

[26] *The Nagasaki Express*, January 28, 1871. From 1876, Richard Lindau served as German consul in Barcelona, Spain, where he opened a popular Japanese art museum in his official residence. He died in Heidelberg, Germany on August 31, 1900, aged sixty-nine.

in Hyōgo (Kobe) and Osaka would be succeeded by a merchant named W. Mourilyan and renamed Mourilyan, Heimann & Co. In Nagasaki, meanwhile, Joseph J. Hunt and Frederick Hellyer, like soldiers picking up fallen flags on the battlefield, would take over the company business as partners but retain the name Alt & Co.

The same day as the above report, Henry J. Hunt and Frederick Hellyer placed an advertisement in the English-language newspaper *The Nagasaki Express* for the sale of the stone bungalow at No. 14 Minamiyamate. The house remained on the market over the following months, apparently vacant. The lack of interest among prospective buyers reflected the stagnant business situation in Nagasaki, but it may also have been due to the scale of the building, too large and grandiose for ordinary purposes, not to mention the spectacular $316 annual land rent demanded by the Japanese government. Hunt and Hellyer also put the office building at No. 7 Ōura up for rent and moved to a smaller building at the rear of the lot, adding to the contraction of activity on the Nagasaki waterfront. A British resident named T. Underwood took over No. 7 Ōura and converted the building into the Western-style Occidental Hotel. As it turned out, Henry J. Hunt and family would, for lack of prospective buyers, be the next inhabitants of the stone bungalow at No. 14 Minamiyamate.

FOR SALE.

FOR SALE.

THE Stone Bungalow formerly occupied by W. J. ALT, Esq.

For particulars apply to

ALT & Co.

Nagasaki, 28th January, 1871.

Henry J. Hunt and Frederick Hellyer posted an advertisement in *The Nagasaki Express* for the sale of the former Alt House at No. 14 Minamiyamate. No serious buyer appeared, nor would the building ever justify the optimism surrounding its construction.

In November 1871, Henry J. Hunt journeyed by steamship and then on foot to Kumamoto, capital of the Higo Domain and a frequent place of business for both Alt & Co. and the now defunct Glover & Co. Hunt reports in his diary that a certain Ora Ke accompanied him on a tour of the famous Kumamoto Castle and joined him for dinner with the Dutch physician C.G. Van Mansvelt, who had been invited to the city the previous year to establish a Western-style hospital. "Ora Ke" is obviously a garbled reference to Ōura Kei (1828-1884), the enterprising Nagasaki merchant who collaborated with foreign counterparts in gathering tea for export and who is remembered today as one of the three great Nagasaki *joketsu* (women of distinction).

The diary entry gives no indication of Ōura's gender, perhaps a reflection of the unusual respect and trust that she had earned in the foreign business community. Hunt mentions that he "talked with Ora about tobacco, 6,000 bales belonging to the Higo Government, but could come to no terms."[27] This anecdote is interesting in that it sheds light on the Tōyama Incident, a scandal that would soon cause a sensation in Kyūshū and wreak financial ruin on Ōura Kei.

As the volume and price of tea declined in the late 1860s, Ōura and other merchants looked to tobacco as a potential new export commodity. In June 1871, she arranged for the purchase of a large stock of tobacco from the former Higo (Kumamoto) Domain, mediating discussions between Alt & Co. and a Kumamoto samurai named Tōyama Ichiya. Alt & Co. paid Tōyama a deposit of 3,000 *ryō* (2,985 Mexican silver dollars)—and Ōura placed her seal on the contract as guarantor—but much to the latter's dismay, Tōyama failed to ship the tobacco to Nagasaki by September as promised.

Over the following months, Ōura attempted without success to make Tōyama honor his promise, at the same time coping with demands from Alt & Co. for the return of the 3,000-*ryō* deposit. Henry J. Hunt is probably lamenting the above dilemma when he reports that he "could come to no terms" with Ōura. In the end, Tōyama was found guilty of fraud in a Japanese court and sentenced to ten years in prison, while Ōura Kei had to shoulder a huge debt that would take years to settle.[28]

------

27 Diary of Henry Joseph Hunt, entry for November 6, 1871.
28 Shigefuji Takeo, *Nagasaki kyoryūchi to gaikokushōnin* (Nagasaki Foreign

The destruction of one of the Alt & Co. tea-firing factories by fire exacerbated concerns among British authorities about the waning importance of tea as an export item from Nagasaki. In July 1872, Nagasaki British Consul Marcus Flowers asked Alt & Co., as leaders in the tea trade, to provide information about the amount of tea leaves sold to foreign merchants during the previous season. The company responded to the request as follows:

> We have endeavored to obtain from the various native merchants the total number of piculs sold by them to foreigners last season. The following are the figures obtained and which we think may be considered fairly reliable.
>
> From Ureshino Hizen district   4,500 piculs
> From Higo district   9,500 piculs
> From Chikugo district   18,000 piculs
> From other districts   3,000 piculs
>
> In addition to the above, about 7,000 piculs of very inferior tea called "bancha" were sold for export to the north of China. A considerable proportion of the teas grown in the surrounding districts is of course used by the natives, but we have no way of estimating the quantity used in this manner.[29]

Hunt Brings his Bride to Nagasaki

Henry J. Hunt writes in his diary that he left Nagasaki for San Francisco via Yokohama in April 1872. The legal proceedings involving Tōyama Ichiya and Ōura Kei were still dragging through Japanese courts as Hunt's ship steamed out of Nagasaki Harbor and set sail across the Pacific Ocean.

After arrival in San Francisco, Hunt traveled by train to Chicago and then on to Montreal via Niagara Falls, engaging in business discussions regarding tea and other Japanese products along the way. On July 4, he boarded the Cunard steamer *Russia* for

---

Settlement and Foreign Merchants), (Kazama Shobō, 1967), 374-99
[29] Alt & Co. to Marcus Flowers, July 9, 1872 (FO 796/55). A term derived from the Chinese word 担, a *picul* is equivalent to about 60 kg or the amount that a laborer can carry in one load.

Liverpool and, back in his homeland, paid a visit to the Alt family at Woburn Park and stayed overnight in their house. He enjoyed meetings with family members and old friends, then crisscrossed the Atlantic Ocean again, traveling around eastern Canada and the United States on business before returning to England in February 1873.

Hunt's diary continues as a mundane record of excursions, stays in hotels and meals with friends until March 8, when he writes—without any previous mention of a romance or engagement—that he had "Married at Highbury. After breakfast went per 3.15 train to Torquay. Stayed at the Torbay Hotel."

Hunt's bride Clara Louisa Hartland was a native of Warrington, Lancashire and about fourteen years his junior.[30] Clara had an older sister, Annie, who never married and lived in the family house in Bedford, west of London, where Henry and Clara would later stay when they were in England. The couple enjoyed a honeymoon in France before catching a series of steamships from Marseilles to Shanghai via the Suez Canal, Singapore and Hong Kong. Hunt sent a telegram to Nagasaki from the latter port, utilizing the submarine cables laid by the Great Northern Telegraph Company only two years earlier. Finally, on June 14, 1873, Henry and Clara arrived in Nagasaki and proceeded to the house at No. 14 Minamiyamate, which had apparently been prepared for them in advance. Reports Hunt in his diary:

> Reached Nagasaki at 1.30 p.m. Found all as much when I left, but the House and Garden done up, and the trees and shrubs considerably grown. Polly [Hunt's pet cockatoo] much as ever and very short of feathers. Hellyer and Wright quite well, likewise Figueiredo, Jewsky, Sangers, Yorozoya, Angoosh, Yataro etc. etc.

With its Western-style appointments, the grand Minamiyamate residence undoubtedly allayed any fears that twenty-one-year-old Clara may have harbored about life in a strange land. She found the colonial-style house comfortably furnished, safely separated from the clamor of the waterfront and Japanese town by

---

[30] From the Census of England and Wales 1911 (RG14/03466/0187/03)

gardens and hillside fences, and offering more than enough space for the brood of children she hoped to raise. The sturdy single-story brick building and coal shed erected at the rear of the main house accommodated a fully equipped kitchen and pantry, as well as rooms for servants furnished in Japanese style with tatami mats and sliding partitions.

Henry and Clara Hunt pose for a photograph with their children and a Japanese amah (nursemaid) in front of No. 14 Minamiyamate circa 1880. (Potter Album, Nagasaki University Library)

William J. Alt officially transferred the lease to No. 14 Minami-yamate to Henry J. Hunt and Frederick Hellyer in September 1873. Although rented nominally by the two business partners, the house served exclusively as a residence for the Hunt family. With Dutch physician W.K.M. van Leeuwen van Duivenbode in attendance, Clara gave birth to a daughter named Edith on December 18, 1873, the first of four children born during the seven-year-long Hunt family stay at No. 14 Minamiyamate. Despite the lengthy period of residence and

Henry J. Hunt's many contributions to international business in Nagasaki, the story of the Hunt family has somehow failed to gain a foothold in local history or to earn mention in modern descriptions of the former Alt House.

The three Alt & Co. employees mentioned in the above diary entry are Frederick Hellyer, Alexander Wright and Jose de Figueiredo. A son of William J. Alt's stepsister Barbara, Hellyer had come to Nagasaki in 1869 at the behest of his uncle to assist in the company business, particularly the export of tea. His brother Thomas, undoubtedly at the introduction of William J. Alt, had been employed as tutor to the children of the daimyo of Tosa. Wright and Figueiredo were clerks and bookkeepers. The remaining names cited by Hunt—Jewsky, Sangers, Yorozoya, Angoosh and Yataro—probably refer to Japanese employees or colleagues. The distorted spellings and lack of full names make the individuals difficult to identify, but "Yataro" may in fact be the Tosa samurai and entrepreneur Iwasaki Yatarō who had associated closely with William J. Alt. If so, it shows that even after renaming his shipping company Mitsubishi Shōkai and beginning his march to the forefront of Japanese industry, Iwasaki Yatarō continued to visit Nagasaki and to maintain his connections with Henry J. Hunt and other foreign merchants.

Disappointing Trade Statistics

As one enterprise after another folded and moved away, Alt & Co. stepped into the vanguard of international business in Nagasaki, leading the trade in tea and other exports and serving as local agent for Lloyd's, the North China Insurance Company and other insurance and shipping concerns. However, neither Henry J. Hunt nor Frederick Hellyer emerged as leaders in the foreign community, preferring to let their compatriot Frederick Ringer head the Municipal Council and various social institutions. The commitment of Hunt and Hellyer to the future of Nagasaki was clearly not as strong as that of Ringer, a native of Norwich, England spearheading an offshoot of Glover & Co. called Holme, Ringer & Co. Indeed, Frederick Ringer would soon surpass all other competitors in Nagasaki and exert a profound

Frederick Hellyer (far left) poses for a photograph with his Nagasaki friends circa 1872. The others are identified (left to right) as Yeend Duer (later an adviser to Mitsubishi), Joseph Longford (British diplomat), Alfred Glover (Thomas Glover's younger brother), and Alexander Hall (Takashima Colliery engineer). (Private Collection)

influence on the development of his adopted hometown. As outlined later in the present work, he and his descendants were also destined to become the last foreign owners of the stone bungalow at No. 14 Minamiyamate.

While Frederick Ringer was striving to open new avenues of trade and industry and pestering Japanese authorities for improvements to infrastructure in the foreign settlement, Henry J. Hunt and Frederick Hellyer spent many a quiet evening lamenting the lull in business and discussing ways to follow in the footsteps of William J. Alt and move on to the greener pastures of Kobe and Yokohama. Their disillusionment with Nagasaki was not unfounded. In an article discussing the state of trade during the year 1873, the editor of *The Nagasaki Express* comments that the statistics are "extremely disappointing," showing a decrease of $370,259 and $923,053 for imports and exports, respectively, over the previous year.[31]

In April 1974, Frederick Hellyer left Japan and traveled to the United States on company business. He returned to Nagasaki in February the following year married to Georgianna Tirrell, the daughter of a Boston merchant whom he had met in California. The couple settled in the house at No. 7 Higashiyamate, overlooking the Ōura commercial district with Minamiyamate and Nagasaki Harbor in the distance.

An Interesting anecdote floats up from the records of the Nagasaki British Consulate in 1875, a time when Thomas B. Glover was still in Nagasaki struggling to tie up the affairs of Glover & Co. In a letter dated May 26, Glover informs British Consul Marcus O. Flowers that he had transferred ownership of the *Argus*—a paddle steamer in use as a tow boat between Nagasaki and Takashima—to Henry J. Hunt.[32] The Takashima Colliery had been sold in its entirety to the Japanese government in January the previous year, but the *Argus* had remained in Glover's possession. A photograph in the Potter Album dated 1873 and preserved at Nagasaki University Library shows an elegant wooden paddle steamer with a caption calling it a "Takashima tow boat." On July 21, 1875, Henry J. Hunt celebrated the birth of his second child, a son named Reginald.

Abode of Bliss

The Nagasaki economy was still in decline in May 1876 when Frederick Hellyer left Nagasaki in preparation for the establishment of Hunt, Hellyer & Co. in Kobe.[33] The new firm announced its inauguration on September 1, 1876, but the partners made frequent trips between the two ports, expanding their business in tea and other exports in Kobe while keeping the Alt & Co. sign up in Nagasaki as a matter of convenience. Henry and Clara Hunt continued to inhabit the house at No. 14 Minamiyamate, giving it the rather odd nickname "Quan-Ran-

---

31 *The Nagasaki Express*, January 28, 1874

32 Thomas B. Glover to Marcus O. Flowers, May 26, 1875 (FO 796/64)

33 *The Rising Sun and Nagasaki Express*, May 13, 1876. Alt & Co. placed an advertisement in the newspaper for the sale of Hellyer's former house at No. 7 Higashiyamate.

Ti," translated on the back of a family photograph as "Abode of Bliss." Although apparently derived from Chinese, the origin of the name remains unclear.

The Occidental Hotel occupying the former Alt & Cp. Office at No. 7 Ōura went bankrupt in late 1876, and notices for the auction of its furniture and appliances appeared in local newspapers. The building found an unexpected new career early the following year as a hospital for soldiers injured in the Satsuma Rebellion, a violent revolt by former samurai disgruntled over their loss of status after the Meiji Restoration. The Satsuma Domain had played a key role in the political revolution that rocked Japan at the end of the Edo Period, but after its rebirth as Kagoshima Prefecture it had begun to raise eyebrows in Tokyo by refusing to pay taxes and allowing its citizens to carry on in their old ways. When the government tried to curb the tide of revolt, the charismatic rebel leader Saigō Takamori declared his intention to appeal to the government in Tokyo and marched out of Kagoshima with an army of some 13,000 troops. Conscripted government regiments trained in the use of European artillery waited along the way. After a blood-drenched siege at Kumamoto Castle, the government army repulsed the ragtag battalion of angry samurai and Saigō committed ritual suicide, bringing an end to the last desperate showdown between the old and the new in Japan.

After the dust settled and the government forces left Nagasaki, Hunt and Hellyer refurbished the former Alt & Co. office at No. 7 Ōura and put it up for sale. In September 1878, the Qing Dynasty government purchased the property and opened Nagasaki's first Chinese Consulate in the historic building.[34]

Henry and Clara Hunt's third child, a daughter named Winifred, was born in the house at No. 14 Minamiyamate in April 1877 and was followed in March 1879 by a son named Geoffrey. Although the focus of Hunt, Hellyer & Co. had shifted from Nagasaki to Kobe, Henry J. Hunt continued to cling to the grand house of wood and

---

[34] One of the oldest buildings in the Nagasaki Foreign Settlement, the former Alt & Co. office at No. 7 Ōura served as a Chinese consulate until 1888, when Holme, Ringer & Co. acquired the property for use as an office. The building remained in the possession of the Ringer family until burning to the ground in a 1947 fire caused by American Occupation personnel.

56

stone on the Minamiyamate hillside and the peaceful if sluggish round of life in Nagasaki. However, it was only a matter of time before he moved over completely to the latter port. The editor of the English-language newspaper *The Rising Sun and Nagasaki Express* summarized the situation and future prospects of Nagasaki at the end of 1877 as follows:

> Within the last two years a considerable reduction has taken place in the number of residents in this settlement. No less than eight firms of greater or less standing have closed, while more than fifty foreigners have left the port, some of those having been replaced, but still leaving a large blank which it is scarcely possible will ever be filled up again... It is not so very long ago that Nagasaki was noted for the number of hotels to be found in it. At the present time the only two which remain, as evidence of the past, are not doing a very thriving business. The closing of the foundry of Messrs. Boyd & Co. and the more recent suspension of the well-known house of Messrs. Gribble & Co., together with the general stagnation of trade since the cessation of war, look gloomy for a no very distant future, and as we glance over the list of residents now here, and the general prospects of such as are but gaining a living, unless a decided re-action ensues, it seems as if it will not be very long before there will be few left beyond consuls, missionaries, telegraph officials, one or two compradores, two or three business houses, and such foreigners as are engaged in government or Japanese employ.[35]

The house at No. 14 Minamiyamate remained in joint possession until June 25, 1878, when Frederick Hellyer transferred his share to Henry J. Hunt. By now, Hunt had risen to prominence as one of the wealthiest and most influential foreign merchants in western Japan. Alt & Co. owned a large number of valuable Nagasaki properties, including the former office at No. 7 Ōura (until September) and other buildings in the rear quarter of the foreign settlement from which Hunt continued to earn revenue. As of the summer of 1878, the properties under the management of Alt & Co. in Nagasaki were: Nos. 7, 8, 18, 19, 20 and 21 Ōura, Nos. 7, 18, 19 and

---

³⁵ *The Rising Sun and Nagasaki Express*, December 8, 1877.

20 Dejima, Nos. 5, 7 and 15 Higashiyamate, and Nos. 14, 29, 30 and 33 Minamiyamate, a land holding unparalleled in the foreign community. Although he had to pay a total of $1,983 in annual land rent to the Japanese government, Hunt enjoyed a lucrative source of income from the rental fees paid by other companies and individuals.[36]

But the time came to pull up stakes and leave Nagasaki. Since the 1880 copies of the English-language newspaper *The Rising Sun and Nagasaki Express* are missing, it is difficult to ascertain the exact date when the Hunt family moved permanently to Kobe, but a photograph of Henry and Clara with other members of the Nagasaki Tennis Club taken in 1880—and the record of the birth of their third son Cecil in Kobe on October 13 the same year—indicate that they removed their belongings from the house at No. 14 Minamiyamate and sailed away from Nagasaki sometime in mid-1880.

Members of the Nagasaki Tennis Club relax during a game on the lawn near Ipponmatsu, the house of Thomas B. Glover at No. 3 Minamiyamate, in 1880. Henry (with beard) and Clara Hunt are seated in the center. Glover is lying on the grass far right. (Potter Album, Nagasaki University Library)

---

[36] FO 796/70/132

Friends with Rudyard Kipling

Henry J. Hunt and Frederick Hellyer parted ways on January 1, 1881, permanently dissolving Alt & Co. and establishing separate companies in Kobe. Both of the new enterprises would thrive over the following years as leaders in the export of tea from Japan.

Henry and Clara Hunt met celebrated British author Rudyard Kipling and his wife Carrie on board the Canadian Pacific liner *Empress of India* sailing from Vancouver to Yokohama in 1892. Catharine Morris Wright describes the encounter as follows:

> Conspicuous as always, the Kiplings met other Empress passengers as the voyage got under way, and sifting them to come up with congenial friends, they discovered a Mr. and Mrs. H. J. Hunt, also headed for Yokohama, also British. Mr. Hunt was the British representative of a London importer who, like all representatives of foreign firms, was making his annual visit to the source of supply. Hunt had begun life twenty years earlier in Alt & Co's Nagasaki office... By 1892, the firm had changed name and personnel... and expanded to Kobe, Yokohama, Shizuoka and Chicago. It was a large and important business and Hunt was by this time no longer young; but he wrote mild and amusing verse which appealed to Kipling and, being generally compatible, before arriving in Japan on the 20th of April, the Hunts had invited the honeymooners to stay with them in Yokohama.[37]

Nagasaki may have provided a topic of common interest in the first-class dining room and bar of the *Empress of India*. Kipling had stopped in Nagasaki during a trip from India to England three years earlier and published an essay on his excursion into the town.[38]

The two couples maintained a friendly correspondence over the following years, and Rudyard Kipling even arranged for the publication of a poem by Henry J. Hunt in the celebrated American

---

[37] Catharine Morris Wright, "How St Nicholas Got Rudyard Kipling And What Happened Then," *Princeton University Library Chronicle*, Volume XXXV, No. 3 (Spring 1974)
[38] Rudyard Kipling, *From Sea to Sea and Other Sketches: Letters of Travel* (London, 1900), I, 326

children's journal *St. Nicholas Magazine*. Copies of the thirteen letters and one telegram sent by Carrie and Rudyard Kipling to Henry and Clara Hunt, plus one letter from Clara Hunt to her husband, can be viewed online.[39]

Henry J. Hunt eventually left the company business in the hands of his two older sons Reginald and Geoffrey. He died in Surrey on September 25, 1918, eighty years of age.

John Hunt won fame as leader of the successful British expedition to Mt. Everest in 1953. The offspring of Henry and Clara's third son Cecil, John learned the techniques of trekking and mountaineering from an early age in India and Europe. After graduating from the Royal Military College, Sandhurst, he received an invitation to lead the first attempt to scale Mt. Everest. Hunt selected two pairs of climbers. The first pair gave up and turned back, but Hunt climbed to 8,350 meters with Da Namgyal Sherpa to deposit equipment for the second pair. On May 29, Edmund Hillary and Sherpa Tenzing Norgay from Nepal reached the world's tallest peak for the first time.

Another descendant of Henry J. Hunt almost disappeared into the mist of history along with other children of mixed race born out of wedlock in nineteenth-century Nagasaki. Only recently did it come to light that Hunt fathered a daughter with a Japanese woman in December 1870, two years before his marriage to Clara Hartland. Unlike other foreigners who turned their backs on their illegitimate offspring, Hunt sent the girl, named Jessie, to England at an early age and arranged for her to be adopted and raised by his sister Mary.[40]

Jessie Hawkesworth Smith later left her mark in history as one of the first female graduates in medicine from the University of Glasgow.[41] However, the name of her Japanese mother and the circumstances of her departure from Nagasaki remain unclear.

---

39 http://www.kiplingjournal.com
40 Personal communication from Jessie's descendants.
41https://pdfs.semanticscholar.org/b347/88b5cdbfd7a0277f6bdd4fc5d78f0a728630.pdf

Chapter 3
American Days

The modern history of Japanese-American relations in Nagasaki begins in May 1859, two months before the official opening of Japan, when U. S. Consul-General Townsend Harris visited the port and appointed an American merchant named John G. Walsh to serve as local consul. The thirty-year-old native of New York established a trading company called Walsh & Co. and served as consul on the side without salary. The building in Hirobaba he used initially as a consulate burned to the ground in December 1859. In 1862, he acquired the lease to No. 12 Higashiyamate and moved the U. S. Consulate there around the same time. The fine Western-style house he built on the lot remains to this day as a National Important Cultural Property.

Like Minamiyamate, the neighborhood known today as Higashiyamate was traditionally part of lands owned by the Ōmura Domain, a stretch of hillside south of the town of Nagasaki inhabited by farmers cultivating vegetables on sun-drenched slopes over-looking Nagasaki Harbor. After the Ansei Five-Power Treaties of 1858 and the opening of the port the following year, the Tokugawa Shogunate divided the hillside into a patchwork of sixteen lots for rental to foreigners. One of the first buildings to appear there was the Episcopal Church (English Church)—the first Protestant place of worship in Japan—erected at No. 11 Higashi-yamate in October 1862 by Koyama Hidenoshin. The representatives of Protestant congregations arrived over the following years and established churches and schools on the hillside, first the Church Mission Society, then the Dutch Reformed Church in America and the Methodist Episcopal Church.

One of the new arrivals was John C. Davison, a Methodist missionary who came to Nagasaki in 1873. Davison appealed to his superiors in the United States for the dispatch of personnel to Nagasaki and in 1879 welcomed Elizabeth Russell and Jennie Gheer, members of the Women's Foreign Missionary Society of the Methodist Episcopal Church. The two women founded a school for girls in their house at No. 16 Higashiyamate, starting classes with only one pupil, and arranged for the construction of a large new building at No. 13 Higashiyamate, the spacious lot reserved, but never used, as a site for the Nagasaki British Consulate.

Elizabeth Russell (left) and Jennie Gheer. Gheer conducted early classes in Western music at No. 14 Minamiyamate. (Kwassui Women's University)

Soon after the Hunt family left Nagasaki in the summer of 1880, Russell and Gheer rented the house at No. 14 Minamiyamate from Henry J. Hunt and converted the building for use as a school while the construction of their new facility proceeded in Higashi-yamate. The eight large rooms of the house provided ample space for classrooms, missionary bedrooms and offices, as well as a dormitory and dining room for pupils. Servants handled the upkeep of buildings and gardens and the preparation of meals in the detached kitchen in the rear. The number of applicants gradually increased, mostly girls from well-to-do Japanese families with connections to the American missionaries. In a report to the Women's Foreign Missionary Society written in late 1881 from No. 14 Minamiyamate, Gheer reported as follows on the school curriculum:

> We teach in our school Japanese, English, music, sewing and fancy work. Of course, we have a Japanese teacher for the Japanese department. The course of study there embraces Japanese and Chinese, Japanese history, Chinese history, universal history, geography, writing, dictation, familiar science and Japanese arithmetic. The English department includes the usual course of study for our home seminaries. We have an excellent matron, who teaches the girls sewing. Our school hours last from eight to twelve A.M. and from one to four P.M. We open with prayers at eight o'clock. Teachers, matron, servants and all are present for that. After this comes the Japanese school until noon, and then the girls gather around the table for dinner. I wish you could see them eat rice with their chopsticks. The Japanese do not sit at a table as we do, but squatting on their mats, their food is brought on little tables, each one having his own. We did not think it would be well to follow that style in school, so we give them a table and chairs, but allow them to use their own dishes, etc. After dinner we have English school. On Saturday the larger girls put their rooms in order and clean them up nicely. We expect those that are large enough to do so to keep their clothing and rooms tidy, and to help the smaller ones. At six o'clock they have supper. About seven we have evening prayer, and after that study hours until nine, when all must retire. Our school-room, as yet, is only an ordinary room in the house, very nice, but not intended for a school-room. It serves the purpose, however, until we get our own house.[42]

In addition to academic and religious subjects, Jennie Gheer taught the rudiments of piano and violin, establishing one of the earliest examples of Western music education in Japan. In a letter the following year, her colleague Elizabeth Russell reported that: "Miss Gheer teaches music, and some of the girls are showing considerable

---

[42] *The Heathen Woman's Friend* (Vol. XIII, December 1881), 134-5

apness in it; they already sing several pieces in English, and five or six of the pupils are getting on nicely in instrumental music."[43]

The new Methodist mission school for girls was erected through donations from the United States and reached completion at No. 13 Higashiyamate in June 1882. One of the largest structures in the Nagasaki Foreign Settlement, the school, named Kwassui Jogakkō (Kwassui Girls School), was disparaged as "ostentatiously conspicuous" by observers writing in the local English-language newspaper but would go on to prosper as a leader of women's education in Japan. Elizabeth Russell and Jennie Gheer continued to rent the former Hunt residence until May 1882, by which time the school enrolment had increased from one to forty-three pupils.[44]

China and Japan Trading Company

The next renter of the stone bungalow at No. 14 Minamiyamate was Edward Rogers, manager of the Nagasaki branch of the China and Japan Trading Company, an American export and import enterprise and commission agency with offices in Nagasaki, Yokohama, Kobe, Osaka, and Shanghai. Although British, Rogers played a leading role in the company business, establishing the Nagasaki office in October 1869 on the choice waterfront lot at No. 4 Ōura, only a few doors north of the Alt & Co. office. With the demise of Glover & Co. and withdrawal of Walsh, Hall & Co. and other enterprises, Roger's company pushed shoulder to shoulder with Alt & Co. to the forefront of foreign trade in Nagasaki.

Rogers remained single for more than a decade, but in March 1881 he married Ellie Hill, a native of Scarsport, Maine, at the British Legation in Tokyo.[45] The couple moved into the house at No. 14 Minamiyamate soon after Elizabeth Russell and Jennie Gheer moved Kwassui Jogakkō to the new school building in Higashiyamate. The American connection may have facilitated the transfer of the lease, but little information, including photographs, memoirs and other documentary evidence, remains to shed light on the stay of the

---

43 *Ibid.* (Vol. XIV, July 1882), 8
44 Kwassui Gakuin, ed., *Kwassui gakuin hyakunenshi* (One Hundred Year History of Kwassui Gakuin) (Nagasaki, 1980), 26-8
45 *The Rising Sun and Nagasaki Express*, April 1, 1882

Rogers family in the house. On January 18, 1883, the China and Japan Trading Company purchased the building and land from Henry J. Hunt and took over the lease, obviously to procure suitable accommodations for the Nagasaki branch manager. Ellie Rogers gave birth to two daughters, Cecile on June 18, 1883 and Margaret on November 12, 1886, while the family was living at No. 14 Minamiyamate.[46]

In addition to selling general merchandise in their store at No. 4 Ōura and serving as ship chandlers and auctioneers, the China and Japan Trading Company imported everything from Cutler, Palmer & Co. wines and spirits to iron bed frames, typewriters and leather products, serving as agents for a long list of foreign insurance and shipping companies and American industries such as the American Ordnance Company of Bridgeport, Connecticut, Selby Smelting & Lead Company of San Francisco, and William Cramp & Sons' Ship and Engine-Building Company of Philadelphia.

In 1889, with Edward Rogers in command, the China and Japan Trading Company secured the lucrative contract to supply all the pipes, hydrants and equipment necessary for the construction of the modern water supply system in Nagasaki, winning over four competitors including three Japanese companies. The successful bid was a fabulous $125,054, some three times the annual municipal budget of Nagasaki.[47] When it began operation in 1891, the Nagasaki Waterworks was Japan's third modern water supply system after Yokohama and Hakodate and the first to feature a dam built exclusively for the conveyance of water. The network of water mains and hydrants brought a dramatic improvement to the health and living conditions of Nagasaki residents and served as a prototype for other waterworks initiated around Japan.[48]

As a fellow member of the small group of American women living in Nagasaki, Ellie Rogers enjoyed a relationship of friendship with the missionaries posted to Kwassui Jogakkō. In January 1890, while her husband was still busy with the import and installment of water supply equipment, she participated in a recital at the school

---

[46] "Births Within the District of the British Consulate at Nagasaki" (FO 796/237)

[47] *The Rising Sun and Nagasaki Express*, June 26, 1889

[48] Japan Commission on Large Dams (ed.), *Dams in Japan: Past, Present and Future* (London: Francis & Taylor Group, 2009), 34-6

along with other foreign residents. A number of Japanese musicians also performed in the recital, evidence of the advancements made in Western music education at the school. Rogers played Mendelssohn's *Song Without Words* on the piano, a performance lauded in the English-language press as, "the most interesting of all, and the lady's execution of this by no means easy piece quite brought down the house."[49]

In 1893, Edward Rogers accepted a transfer to Yokohama as manager of the China and Japan Trading Company branch office in that port. Upon departure from Nagasaki, he hired a local auctioneer to preside over a public sale at No. 14 Minamiyamate, offering the "usual line of household furniture" in a notice posted in the English-language newspaper. The frequency of auctions of this sort throughout the foreign settlement period shows that residents preferred to sell their tables, chairs, beds, carpets and other belongings instead of hauling them from one station to another. The timing of the September 1893 auction indicates that the Rogers family vacated the house around that date and left Nagasaki for their new life in Yokohama.

Edward Rogers did not remain long with the China and Japan Trading Company. In 1894, he joined the Standard Oil Company of New York and became local manager at Yokohama. Although not recorded in Japan from 1901 to 1906, he resurfaces in 1907 as managing director of the Union Estate & Investment Company, Builders and Contractors, living with his wife and two daughters at No. 108 on the Yokohama Bluff. He died in 1929 and was buried in the Yokohama Foreigners' Cemetery.[50]

Nagasaki U. S. Consulate

William H. Abercrombie arrived in Nagasaki in August 1890 to succeed John M. Birch as American Consul in this port. A practicing physician prior to his appointment, the New York native had no experience in public service or relations with Japan. In fact, his principal qualification seems to have been a recommendation from his uncle, the illustrious Admiral Robert W. Shufeldt, a navy hero who had

---

[49] *The Rising Sun and Nagasaki Express*, January 29, 1890
[50] http://www.meiji-portraits.de/meiji_portraits_r.html

represented the United States in signing a treaty of amity with Korea in 1882 and who had friends in the newly elected Republican administration. Abercrombie's appointment points to a fundamental difference between the American and British consuls at the time: the latter were members of the Japan Consular Service who had started their careers as student interpreters and worked at various posts in Japan, Korea and Formosa (Taiwan) until retirement; the former were usually chosen on the basis of political connections, not experience in diplomacy or Japan studies, and served short terms in only one location.[51]

Abercrombie was single and took up residence alone in the U. S. Consulate at No. 7 Minamiyamate, a wooden building dating back to the early days of the foreign settlement. Whether out of homesickness or distain for his new surroundings, he began to suffer from mental problems almost as soon as he opened the shutters on his office windows. His dislike may have been aggravated by the cholera epidemic that swept through Nagasaki and environs during the summer of his arrival, claiming 2,500 lives before finally subsiding in November. Charles A. Arnold, a British physician practicing in Nagasaki and serving as Abercrombie's personal doctor, jotted a note on a sheet of Nagasaki Club letter paper, recommending that the American consul be allowed to take a leave of absence. Wrote Arnold: "Dr. W.H. Abercrombie has been under my care for the last 6 months suffering from extreme nervous debility. In my opinion a thorough change preferably to the United States is absolutely necessary for the re-establishment of his health."[52]

The absence of a vice consul to serve as substitute impeded Abercrombie's efforts to return home on leave. Before submitting a request for a sixty-day leave of absence in May 1892, he appointed the Swiss-born American physician Charles E. Amuat to serve as vice consul. The plan to leave Nagasaki was thwarted, however, when

---

[51] The U. S. consular system was reorganized in 1906, after which time consuls were chosen from a pool of foreign service officials with experience in diplomatic service. The first consul assigned to Nagasaki after the 1906 reforms was George H. Scidmore, a long-time official at the U. S. Consulate in Yokohama.
[52] March 14, 1891. "Despatches from U. S. Consuls in Nagasaki, Japan," NARA Record Group 59, M131, Roll 5, 0351

Amuat died of a sudden illness three days before receiving his official appointment. Abercrombie tried again in December, this time choosing his personal physician Charles A. Arnold (although British) for the post of vice consul and submitting the request for leave the same day. On June 3, 1893, the beleaguered consul was finally able to escape from Nagasaki and return to the United States.[53]

Arnold posted a notice in the August 28, 1893 issue of *The Rising Sun and Nagasaki Express* announcing the move to No. 14 Minamiyamate (also referred to as Naminohira or Namenohira Hill at the time).

Before leaving, Abercrombie arranged to rent the former residence of Edward Rogers at No. 14 Minamiyamate—which remained in the possession of the China and Japan Trading Company—for use as the U. S. Consulate. The contract was concluded in August during Abercrombie's absence, leaving it to Charles A. Arnold to post a notice in the English-language newspaper *The Rising Sun and Nagasaki Express*.

Charles A. Arnold had graduated in medicine from Aberdeen University and arrived in Nagasaki in 1886 at the age of twenty-eight to open a private practice in the foreign settlement. His surgical skills caught the attention of Japanese residents, and in 1888 he was engaged by the government-run Nagasaki Hospital to teach students and perform operations. His first duty in the new U. S. Consulate at No. 14 Minamiyamate was the controversial questioning and trial of an American shipmaster named Lorin Groth.

---

[53] Ibid., RG 59, M131, Roll 5, 0472.

While his ship docked at Kuchinotsu (a small port on the Shimabara Peninsula near Nagasaki) to take on a cargo of coal, Groth had sent a sick crewmember to Nagasaki to see a doctor. The doctor pronounced the man unfit to go to sea and referred him to U. S. Vice Consul Charles A. Arnold, who forwarded a telegram to Kuchinotsu asking Groth to come to Nagasaki with the man's discharge papers and luggage. When the shipmaster failed to respond, Arnold sent deputy marshal Frank Nevells to Kuchinotsu with an arrest warrant. Groth agreed to visit the U. S. Consulate but refused to produce the warrant. Arnold ordered Nevells to search his person. In the ensuing scuffle, Groth was pushed to the floor of the courtroom and only allowed to stand after the warrant had been retrieved from his boot. Arnold conducted the discharge procedures without further mishap, imposing a token fine of one dollar for contempt of court. He even tried to mollify any hurt feelings by serving beer to his visitors in the consulate reception room. But the issue did not end there. Groth later wrote an impassioned letter to *The San Francisco Bulletin*, complaining about the violence suffered in Arnold's courtroom and vowing to appeal the case in Washington. His letter was reprinted in newspapers throughout the country under the title "Queer Case at Nagasaki," the principal queerness apparently being, not the violence, but the fact that a Briton had passed sentence on an American citizen in a U. S. consular court.[54]

William H. Abercrombie returned to Japan in September 1893 and wrote a letter to Josiah Quincy, Assistant Secretary of State, reporting the consular accounts up to the end of the month and mentioning the fact that, due to the dilapidation of the premises at No. 7 Minamiyamate, he had moved the consulate to the former Rogers residence at No. 14 Minamiyamate.

Writes the consul: "Fortunately I was able to secure the premises belonging to an American firm—the China and Japan Trading Company, in which its manager occupied, and he was leaving Nagasaki at the time, which is situated at No. 14 Naminohira Hill [Minamiyamate] and on same terms as the old place. The new

---

[54] The letter was also carried in *The Japan Gazette* and reprinted in the December 13, 1893 issue of *The Rising Sun and Nagasaki Express*. Captain Groth would later succeed in winning back the fine and other expenses incurred in Nagasaki.

premises are more eligibly situated and more accessible and convenient in every way."[55]

In response to a query from the Department of State, Abercrombie followed up the report with a list of answers to questions about the new consulate and a floor plan showing how the rooms were being used. Written in the consul's own hand, the letter and floor plan shed a valuable light on the state of the former Alt House during its career as the U. S. Consulate in Nagasaki:

> 1st. The amount expended annually by me for rent of office is six hundred dollars (U. S. Gold).
>
> 2nd. The number, dimensions and location of rooms is shown in accompanying diagram.
>
> 3rd. I occupy for private purposes one room marked bedroom in diagram and room marked reception room partially as dining room. As an offset to this I pay for heating, lighting, building and for services of janitor and messenger.
>
> 4th. I reside in consular building. The building now occupied as the American Consulate is owned by the China and Japan Trading Company, an American company. It is a building well adapted for its present purpose. On account of the scarcity of foreign houses in Nagasaki and injuries received in typhoon by building lately occupied as consulate, I consider myself very fortunate in being able to secure the present location.[56]

The floor plan enclosed in the letter sent to the Department of State shows that, in the daytime, Abercrombie shared the house at No. 14 Minamiyamate with his interpreter Simão R. de Souza and deputy marshal (later marshal) Frank Nevells, both of whom had offices in rooms at the rear of the house. A "janitor and messenger" are the only domestic staff mentioned, but the category undoubtedly included a number of maids, cooks and gardeners employed to maintain the building and cater to everyday needs. Vice Consul

---

[55] William H. Abercrombie to Josiah Quincy, September 30, 1893, NARA, RG59, M131, Roll 5, 0482.
[56] Ibid., November 19, 1893, NARA, RG59, M131, Roll 5, 0492-3.

Charles A. Arnold did not have a separate office in the consulate. Only William H. Abercrombie stayed overnight, occupying the bedrooms adjacent to his office, listening to the songs of insects in the surrounding trees, and apparently preferring hermit-like solitude to social interaction.

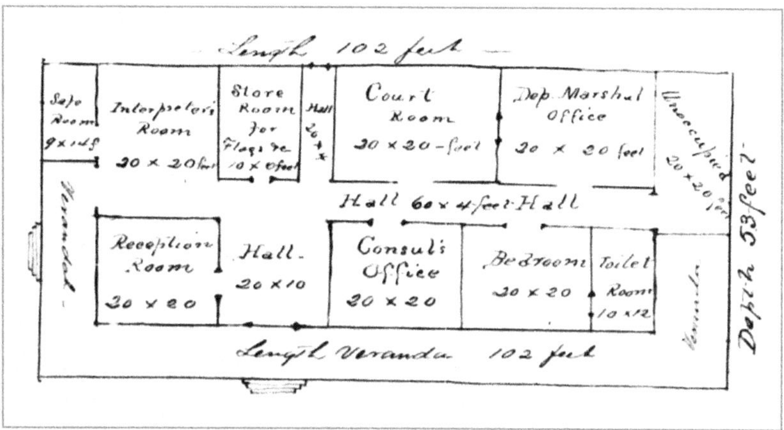

Abercrombie's hand-drawn floor plan provides a rough layout of rooms in the U. S. Consulate at No. 14 Minamiyamate.

Interpreter and Marshal

Born in Macao and educated in Bombay, Portuguese national Simão R. de Souza arrived in Nagasaki in 1872 to assist a compatriot running an English-language newspaper and print shop. He met a Japanese woman named Hamamoto Shito from Shimabara and fathered a child with her in 1880. Formally married in a ceremony at Ōura Catholic Church in 1885, the couple went on to have fifteen children, eight of whom died tragically in infancy or childhood. From the year of his marriage, de Souza filled the well-paid position of interpreter and clerk at the U. S. Consulate, serving two successive consuls prior to the arrival of William H. Abercrombie in Nagasaki.

Frank Nevells came to Nagasaki in 1883 and found employment with a fellow American merchant and ship-chandler named Rodney H. Powers. While still employed by Powers, he accepted the role of deputy marshal in the U. S. Consulate, a job that mainly entailed the policing of the American sailors who came ashore on leave and who either patronized the sleazy taverns lining Sagarimatsu Creek or ventured into the brothel district in the Japanese town. The rules of extraterritoriality, set out by the Ansei Five-Power Treaties of 1858, ensured that any American causing a disturbance in Nagasaki would be arrested by the marshal and tried, not in a Japanese court, but in the courtroom of the U. S. Consulate.

Despite his role in maintaining public order, Nevells did not enjoy universal popularity or respect. In 1893, he was accused of smuggling Japanese women overseas for the purpose of prostitution, causing a flurry of indignation in the Japanese community even though he was later declared innocent in the consular court. His reputation in the foreign settlement was not much better. Wrote the editor of the English-language newspaper *The Nagasaki Shipping List* (September 14, 1895), reporting Nevells' return from a trip to Yokohama: "His beaming smile, on landing, was difficult to account for at first until it was discovered that he had brought back with him the two dollars he had started off with, in addition to a fistful of unclaimed poker chips."

Model for Mr. Sharpless?

Soon after resuming his post in Nagasaki in the autumn of 1893, William H. Abercrombie presided over a wedding ceremony at Kwassui Girls School. American Methodist minister Irvin H. Correll conducted the service, joining two young missionaries in matrimony. Correll, who served as principal of the Methodist mission school for boys in Nagasaki, would go on to enjoy a measure of fame, not for success in winning Japanese converts, but for *Madame Butterfly*, a story set in Nagasaki and published in a New York magazine by his brother-in-law John Luther Long. In the making of the novelette, Long (who never came to Japan himself) borrowed many scenes and characters from *Madame Chrysanthéme*, the best-selling *comédie japonaise* published by French author Pierre Loti in 1887, but he also gathered information about Nagasaki from his sister Jennie Correll, whose sojourn in Nagasaki coincided closely with that of William H. Abercrombie. In fact, Long may have modeled the American consul of his novelette, the dour Mr. Sharpless, after descriptions of Abercrombie penned in letters from his sister.

The U. S. Consul Mr. Sharpless (left) depicted in an illustration from the opera *Madame Butterfly*. Converted into a stage play by David Belasco and later an opera by Giacomo Puccini, the tale of a Japanese girl betrayed by an American naval officer continues to this day to enchant audiences around the world. (Private collection)

The wedding party at Kwassui Girls School was more the exception than the rule in Abercrombie's social life. The U. S. Consul seldom participated in the various organizations of the foreign settlement, nor did he engage in friendly encounters with Japanese residents. He stayed in the house at No. 14 Minamiyamate, fulfilling mundane duties during the day and spending nights alone in his bedroom. Vexed by poor physical and mental health, he waited constantly for an opportunity to abscond, if not a sixty-day leave in the United States then at least a thirty-day domestic vacation. His hopes were regularly dashed, however, by the death or resignation of his vice consul, who would have to be there to substitute for him.

John C. Smith Acquires the Lease

The lease to No. 14 Minamiyamate changed hands in 1894. In a letter dated March 21 the same year, Abercrombie notified the British Consulate of the transfer of the lease from the China and Japan

Trading Company to John Carrick Smith.[57] A native of Ayr, Scotland, Smith came to Nagasaki in the 1860s to work for Glover & Co. In 1870, he joined Holme, Ringer & Co. as partner and went on to win respect as a leading resident of the Nagasaki Foreign Settlement.[58] The lack of any other connection to the house suggests that he acquired the lease to No. 14 Minamiyamate simply as an investment.

Much of William H. Abercrombie's time in early 1894 was occupied by court hearings and communication with Japanese authorities regarding a wayward American resident named George Lake, who had been deported from Japan in 1871 but snuck back into the country in early 1893. The governor of Nagasaki informed Abercrombie that the deportation order was still in effect, but Lake managed to evade the edict and remain in Nagasaki until January 1894, when he was arrested and his property confiscated and sold off to pay his debts and legal costs. Abercrombie's frustration with Lake continued over the following months: the American outlaw acquiesced to deportation to Shanghai on three occasions but returned to Nagasaki each time. It was not until July 1894 that he finally gave up and stayed in Korea, allowing Abercrombie to close the case.

The U. S. Consul had barely finished with George Lake when Charles A. Arnold died in his residence at No. 15 Minamiyamate. Only thirty-six years old at the time, the British physician left a wife and two young daughters. The writer of an obituary in the local English-language newspaper reports that Arnold died under "sad and sudden circumstances" but mentions no illness. Whether the writer is alluding to suicide, however, cannot be discerned from this or any other document. Arnold's widow put the family belongings up for auction and returned to England soon thereafter.

Early the following year, Abercrombie recommended Herbert Blackburn for the post of U. S. Vice Consul. Like Arnold, Blackburn was a British physician serving as a medical practitioner in the foreign settlement and assisting the consul as a medical advisor. However, tragedy struck again. Blackburn's thirty-three-year-old wife

---

[57] W.H. Abercrombie to A.M. Chalmers, March 21, 1894 (FO 796/127)

[58] John C. Smith appears along with Ringer and William J. Alt in the photograph taken after the Nagasaki Regatta in May 1866 (see p. 34). Smith returned permanently to Scotland in 1900.

Emily died of a sudden illness on March 3, 1895 and was buried next to Charles A. Arnold at Sakamoto International Cemetery. Blackburn remained in Nagasaki for a few months, but he returned to England with his two infant children in November, once again vacating the post of U. S. Vice Consul.

The six-by-six-meter courtroom at No. 14 Minamiyamate saw an unprecedented burst of activity in the summer of 1895—and William H. Abercrombie faced his greatest challenge to date as judge—when an American sailor on shore leave in Nagasaki was charged with the murder of a Japanese citizen.

The Trial of John Thomas Bush

The war between Japan and China over conflicting interests in Korea ended in victory for Japan and the signing of the Treaty of Shimonoseki on April 17, 1895. The treaty compelled China to recognize Korea as an independent country, to cede territory including the Liaodong Peninsula and Taiwan, and to give Japan commercial rights similar to those enjoyed by Britain and the United States. On June 16, a grand celebration was held in the park near Suwa Shinto Shrine to pay tribute to Japanese soldiers and sailors, and thousands of people poured into Nagasaki from surrounding districts. The festivities included musical presentations, dances, displays of martial arts and fireworks. The revelers consumed enough saké and whisky to float a small gunboat as the merriment continued into the night. Thomas B. Glover, a staunch Japanophile, illuminated his house on the Minamiyamate hillside to celebrate the occasion.[59]

The cruiser U.S.S. *Yorktown* happened to be anchored in Nagasaki Harbor at the time, and many of the crew, granted shore leave, went to Suwa Shinto Shrine to enjoy the entertainments. One was a young sailor named John Thomas Bush who, while walking back through downtown Nagasaki with a companion, got into a brawl in the Nishi-Hamanomachi neighborhood. In the chaos, a blacksmith named Kamimura Kanjirō was slashed in the chest and abdomen with a razor and died an hour later from loss of blood. Still holding the blood-smeared weapon, Bush was arrested and marched off to the Japanese police station on charges of murder.

---

[59] *The Rising Sun and Nagasaki Express,* June 19, 1895

Visitors crowd around the stairs at the front gate to Suwa Shinto Shrine during the autumn Kunchi Festival circa 1900. The spacious grounds of the shrine served as a venue for various celebrations over the years. Picture postcard. (Private collection)

In accordance with the rules of extraterritoriality, the American sailor faced trial in the U. S. consular courtroom at No. 14 Minamiyamate, with William H. Abercrombie presiding.

Abercrombie enlisted four American residents to serve as assessors and called seventeen witnesses including Japanese bystanders, policemen and physicians. After all the testimony had been aired, he found Bush guilty, not of murder, but of manslaughter, the lighter verdict based on the fact that 1) Bush had been carrying the razor only to have it sharpened in town, that 2) the Japanese crowd, although unarmed, was agitated by the raucous celebration and excited by alcohol, and that 3) some of the prosecution testimony was ambiguous and contradictory. Two of the assessors opposed the decision, but Edwin Dun, U. S. Envoy to Japan, sanctioned it in a later deposition, and Bush was sentenced as prescribed by Abercrombie to three years in the American jail in Yokohama and a fine of one thousand dollars. While reporting in detail on the case, Japanese newspapers did not criticize the light sentence or mention any measure on the part of the U. S. Consulate to compensate the victim's family.

W.H. Abercrombie Purchases No. 14 Minamiyamate

The conviction and imprisonment of John Thomas Bush coincided with a sea change in Japan's relationship with the United States and other powers. In November 1894, while war raged between Japan and China, the United States followed the example of Britain and signed a new treaty of commerce and navigation with Japan. Effective July 17, 1899, the revised treaty called for an end to extraterritoriality and a restoration of Japanese autonomy in customs tariffs and other international contracts. Japan reciprocated by agreeing to honor the leases still in effect in the foreign settlements and allowing the citizens of treaty nations to travel, reside, and do business anywhere they wanted in Japan. Writing from his office at No. 14 Minamiyamate, William H. Abercrombie weighed in on the subject, praising Japan for its success in the project of modernization and adding his opinion that: "Once aroused to a realization of the work necessary to be accomplished before she could take her place among the great and progressive nations of the world, [Japan] has rested neither day nor night to elevate herself in all respects to their level. History furnishes no example of such wonderful and rapid progress."[60]

The U. S. Consul continued his struggle to find a vice consul—and return home on leave—well into the following year. He recommended William Devine, a Briton employed as an accountant at the Mitsubishi Nagasaki Shipyard, but the appointment was delayed in the face of protests from American residents, none of whom, however, stepped forward to take the job. Samuel D. Hepburn, an American employee of the Standard Oil Company of New York, volunteered in time for Abercrombie to take a vacation but had to quit after only two weeks because of pressing company duties, thus forcing the luckless U. S. Consul to return to Nagasaki.

Shortly after returning to his duties, William H. Abercrombie arranged for the purchase of the land and buildings at No. 14 Minamiyamate from John C. Smith. Oddly enough, the transaction is not mentioned in any of the letters or other documents preserved in the archive entitled *Despatches from U. S. Consuls in Nagasaki, Japan,*

---

[60] William H. Abercrombie to Edwin F. Ulil, Assistant Secretary of State, February 23, 1895. (NARA, RG59, M131, Roll 6, 0100-0143)

nor in the English-language newspapers or the notifications sent from the consulates to Japanese authorities. The entry in the British Consulate land register, dated March 22, 1897 and signed by British Consul Joseph H. Longford, reads as follows: "Transferred by deed of conveyance purporting to have been executed by John Carrick Smith March 20th, 1897 and registered in the register of deeds as No. 45 Page 45 March 22nd, 1897 to W.H. Abercrombie, a United States citizen."[61] The phrasing suggests that the sale of the property was concluded privately by the two parties and that the British consul was informed by word of mouth only. It would not be the last time that the stone bungalow at No. 14 Minamiyamate changed ownership under dubious circumstances.

Ignoring the protests from other American residents, Abercrombie pushed through the appointment of William Devine as U. S. Vice Consul and submitted a formal request for a sixty-day leave to the Unites States starting from April 1, 1897, accompanied by a medical certificate confirming his nervous debility.[62] William Devine had been living in Nagasaki since his employment in 1884 as an accountant at the Mitsubishi Nagasaki Shipyard. A founding member of the Nagasaki Masonic Lodge, he fulfilled the duties of U. S. Vice Consul over the next five months, commuting to Minamiyamate from his house in Akunoura near the shipyard.

Charles B. Harris

William H. Abercrombie returned to his office in Nagasaki on September 1, 1897, several weeks late. The following month, he received news that Charles B. Harris, president of the Indiana State Board of Agriculture, had been appointed to replace him as U. S. Consul in Nagasaki. While preparing for departure, Abercrombie posted an advertisement for the sale of the house at No. 14 Minamiyamate on the front page of *The Nagasaki Press*.[63] The iconic building quickly found a buyer in the person of British widow Kate Barff, who took over the lease as of January 4, 1898. Before Charles

---

[61] FO 796/206/61

[62] William H. Abercrombie to William W. Rockhill, Assistant Secretary of State, February 12, 1897. (NARA, RG59, M131, Roll 6, 01203)

[63] *The Nagasaki Press*, November 27, 1897

B. Harris had a chance to intervene, Abercrombie promised Barff that the U. S. government would continue to use No. 14 Minamiyamate as a consulate and pay her 1,800 yen per annum for rent.

Like William H. Abercrombie, the fifty-five-year-old Charles B. Harris was a civilian with no previous experience in diplomacy or Japan studies. He arrived in Nagasaki with his wife and daughter on January 12, settled into No. 14 Minamiyamate and took up the duties of U. S. Consul the following week. William H. Abercrombie's departure, meanwhile, went mostly undocumented. Despite the retiring consul's eight-year term of public service, local newspapers do not mention any farewell party or other demonstration of friendship, nor did the governor of Nagasaki receive word in writing of his withdrawal.

Abercrombie married a woman named Emelie Seyfert after returning to the United States but committed suicide at the Stoneleigh Court Apartments, Washington D.C. on September 6, 1907, aged sixty-five. *The New York Times* carried a short obituary entitled "W.H. Abercrombie – A Suicide – Former New York Physician, Once Consul at Nagasaki."[64]

One of Charles B. Harris' first initiatives as consul was to nullify his predecessor's appointment of William Devine as U. S. Vice Consul and to replace him with E.R. Fulkerson, an American missionary stationed in Nagasaki.[65] He also fired Simão R. de Souza, who had been serving as the consulate interpreter and clerk for more than ten years, pointing out that he was "not American" and insisting that he was incompetent as an interpreter. De Souza appealed his case to American authorities and demanded compensation but eventually took up a new position with the U. S. Army Depot in Nagasaki.

Harris also dismissed Frank Nevells, who had served in the consulate for nine years, and replaced him with a foreign service official. Nevells died in 1925 in the Japanese neighborhood of Jūnin-machi. After cremation, his ashes were interred at a nearby Buddhist temple, in a cemetery lot belonging to his Japanese housekeeper that can no longer be identified today.

---

[64] *The New York Times*, September 7, 1907
[65] William Devine died at his residence in Akunoura on July 7, 1899 at the age of sixty-four and was buried at Sakamoto International Cemetery.

Simão R. de Souza (left) poses for a photograph with his son Joseph and an unidentified associate. De Souza died on January 6, 1904 at the age of sixty-seven and was buried at Sakamoto International Cemetery. (Private collection)

The End of Extraterritoriality

The last criminal case tried in the U. S. Consulate courtroom at No. 14 Minamiyamate was one of the most serious in the history of the Nagasaki Foreign Settlement. An American barkeeper named John Kelly was accused of shooting and killing an American drifter named Owen Gannon on the evening of May 15, 1898.

Running for more than seventy pages in the consular archive, the transcript of the proceedings reads like a tale of violence and lawlessness in some backwater saloon in the Wild West. Gannon was a former sailor discharged dishonorably from the U. S. Navy and living as a drifter in Nagasaki. Kelly, also a former sailor, operated a tavern at No. 35 Ōura, one in a row of seedy alehouses teetering on the edge of Sagarimatsu Creek and catering to the crews of foreign warships and merchantmen arriving daily in Nagasaki Harbor. Gannon visited Kelly's tavern with three friends, worse for drink and already bruised from a fight earlier in the day. After his companions left, he demanded a drink but was refused because he had no money.

Enraged, he threatened to hit Kelly with a spittoon, whereupon the latter pulled a revolver from a drawer and fired three shots. Two of the bullets disappeared harmlessly into the wall of the saloon, but the third hit Gannon in the chest and severed his pulmonary artery, causing the internal bleeding that would prove fatal.

At the trial, Kelly pleaded not guilty, testifying that the revolver had discharged accidentally when he placed it on the bar counter. However, Charles B. Harris and his four assessors declared Kelly guilty of first-degree murder and sentenced him to death. In an addendum dated July 9, 1898, Harris announced that he had reduced the sentence to life imprisonment on the basis of instructions from the American government. While Kelly waited in the British Consulate jail at No. 6 Ōura, a retrial was ordered and resulted in a further reduction of the sentence to seven years for manslaughter. Ultimately, the barkeeper served only one year in jail, a farcical outcome that exposed the absurdity of the consular court and presaged the demise of extraterritoriality and other special privileges for foreigners in Japan.

Since his predecessor had signed a contract to rent the house at No. 14 Minamiyamate for one year from January 1898, Charles B. Harris had no choice but to continue living there with his wife and daughter. At the end of the year, however, he arranged to move the consulate and his private residence to No. 4 and 5 Ōura, waterfront buildings close to the foreign settlement business district. The Harris family was already living at No. 5 Ōura at the end of December 1898 when Japanese authorities conducted a census of foreign residents.[66] In a letter dated January 3, 1899, Harris reported the move as a *fait accompli* and provided a description and floor plan of the new consular premises, pointing out that the combined rent was 1,560 yen per annum, considerably less than the 1,800 yen demanded by Kate Barff for No. 14 Minamiyamate. Continues Harris:

> My reasons for a removal of the Consulate are that the former place is situated on a high hill at a distance of nearly half a mile from the business portion and the foreign settlement and from the landing that is generally used by people coming from vessels.

---

[66] *Nagasaki kyoryūchi gaikokujin meibo III* (List of Foreign Residents of the Nagasaki Foreign Settlement, Vol.3), 241

In addition to the inconvenience of distance is the further objection that anyone who is at all pressed for time or is not physically strong must pay twenty sen to reach the house, and from thirty to fifty sen for a round trip by jinrikisha. All who had to do business at the consulate, ship captains, agents, merchants etc. continually and loudly complained at the distance, and at being put to this apparently needless expense. A very serious objection is that the house is built of stone, is very old, has never since it was built been dry in the damp climate, and is so placed behind and under a high hill as to continue [being] damp and to be an unhealthy place in which to have an office or to reside. The books, papers and archives were at all times more or less damp, and after they had been there a short time they became musty and remained so. The reason why I remained there was that I had no other place to which I could take the consulate.[67]

The Eccentric Mrs. Barff

The departure of the Harris family marked the end of No. 14 Minamiyamate as an American diplomatic station and consular residence. The house returned to the hands of its owner and leaseholder, Kate Barff, a British widow living alone in the house called Cliff Field on the adjacent lot at No. 15 Minamiyamate.

A native of West Sussex, England, Kate Barff (nee Katherine Anne Clayton) married at an early age and accompanied her husband Samuel to Eastern Europe and later Greece, where the latter served as British vice consul in the port of Patras. She was the mother of three sons and a daughter when the family arrived in Hong Kong in 1870. Samuel took up the position of assistant postmaster in the colony, later rising through the ranks of the civil service as deputy registrar and accountant for the Supreme Court.[68] In an 1884 document, the Barff family is listed as living in a house called "The

---

[67] Charles B. Harris to David J. Hill, Assistant Secretary of State, January 3, 1899, NARA, RG59, M131, Roll 6, 01435-6. Harris remained in Nagasaki until 1907, when he was appointed U. S. consul to Reichenberg, Austria.

[68] *The Chronicle and Directory for China and Japan*, 1868 to 1893 issues

Hut" on Castle Road in an affluent neighborhood of Hong Kong.[69] In April the same year, Kate's daughter Lucy died at the age of nineteen and was buried in the Happy Valley Cemetery, where her gravestone can still be seen today.

Shipping intelligence in the English-language newspapers shows Samuel and Kate Barff arriving in Nagasaki from Shanghai aboard the steamship *Yokohama-maru* on April 27, 1894. The couple's motivation in choosing Nagasaki as a place of retirement remains unclear, although they were certainly not alone. Many other foreign visitors were calling at the port and deciding to stay, captivated by Nagasaki's moderate climate, beautiful scenery and peaceful multinational community. An added amenity was Shimabara, a hot-spring-dotted peninsula near Nagasaki gaining popularity as a summer resort among the well-heeled expatriates of Shanghai and Hong Kong. The census conducted by Japanese authorities at the end of 1894 shows Samuel and Kate living in the Higashiyamate neighborhood of the Nagasaki Foreign Settlement.

Still another attending factor may have been the Sino-Japanese War, a bloody clash between Japan and China that raged in regions close to Nagasaki from July 1894 to April 1895. Lionel C. Barff, the youngest son of Samuel and Kate, stayed with his parents in Nagasaki while serving as a correspondent for *The London Illustrated News* and submitted numerous sketches to the magazine. Before returning to Victoria, Canada (where he had been working previously as a mining broker and art teacher) in May 1895, he held an exhibition in his parents' Higashiyamate residence, including paintings of Unzen, Aba and other areas near Nagasaki that the writer of an article in the English-language newspaper praised as displaying "a delicate and refined scheme of colour wedded to a keen sense of composition."[70]

In early 1897, Samuel and Kate Barff acquired the lease to No. 15 Minamiyamate and the large house known among foreign residents as Cliff Field, situated on the hillside to the south of the U. S. Consulate at No. 14 Minamiyamate. Samuel's health deteriorated over the following months. He died on August 25 the same year, aged

---

[69] *Private Residences of the Principal Government Officials, the leading Merchants, the Consuls, Professional men, and Justices of the Peace*
(https://gwulo.com/node/7062)
[70] *The Rising Sun and Nagasaki Express*, May 1, 1895

sixty-nine, and was buried at Sakamoto International Cemetery. The census conducted by Japanese authorities at the end of 1897 shows Kate Barff living alone at No. 15 Higashiyamate.

As outlined above, Kate Barff bought the house at No. 14 Minamiyamate on January 4, 1898, assured by William H. Abercrombie that the American government would continue to rent the property for use as the U. S. Consulate. The annual rent of 1,800 yen was a huge sum at the time, twice as high as the rental fee Abercrombie had paid earlier to the China and Japan Trading Company. When she realized in December 1898 that Abercrombie's successor Charles B. Harris intended to move the consulate to the Ōura waterfront, Barff posted an advertisement in *The Nagasaki Press* offering to sell or rent the bungalow at No. 14 Minamiyamate, with the rather odd postscript that "if preferred" she was willing to rent or sell No. 15 Minamiyamate (Cliff Field) instead.[71] The departure of the Harris family clearly threw her into a quandary about what to do with the two expensive properties in her possession. The results of the advertisement were not published, but related documents indicate that she found renters for Cliff Field and moved her own place of residence to No. 14 Minamiyamate. In February 1899, she held an auction of household furniture at No. 15 Minamiyamate, including several of her son's oil paintings.

TO LET OR FOR SALE.

The BUNGALOW.

No. 14, Naminohira Hill,

at present occupied by the U.S. Consul. With POSSESSION February 1st, 1899, or, if preferred, the next Lot No. 15, CLIFF FIELD.

Apply to R.H. POWERS for Particulars.

Nagasaki, 3rd December, 1898.

Kate Barff posted an advertisement for the sale of No. 14 Minamiyamate in *The Nagasaki Press.*

---

[71] *The Nagasaki Press*, December 3, 1898.

Nagasaki Prefecture conducted a final census of foreign residents on December 31, 1899, a few months after the abolition of extraterritoriality and the absorption of the foreign settlement into the city. The census shows Kate Barff living at No. 14 Minamiyamate with her younger brother Thorton Clayton.[72] Ernest A. Measor, a young British clerk working for Holme, Ringer & Co., is also listed as living at No. 14 Minamiyamate with his wife and son, but the entry probably refers to a house on a subdivided section of the property.[73] By that time, No. 15 Minamiyamate had also undergone subdivisions as a result of the surging demand for Western-style accommodations in the foreign settlement after the Sino-Japanese War.

Kate Barff received news in 1900 that her son Lionel, who had traveled to northern China to cover the Boxer Rebellion as a special correspondent for *The Illustrated London News*, had fallen gravely ill while following the march of allied troops from Tientsin to Beijing. She boarded a steamship to Shanghai, intending to rush to his bedside, but, upon landing, learned of his death due to typhoid fever.[74]

After the tragic death of her son, Kate Barff became an increasingly eccentric presence on the Minamiyamate hillside, engaging in squabbles with Frederick Ringer and other neighbors over property boundaries, submitting peculiar messages to the editor of *The Nagasaki Press*, and bothering the British consul with trivial complaints. In September 1901, she wrote to Nagasaki Prefecture Governor Arakawa Yoshitarō (addressing him incorrectly as Harakawa) announcing that she was paying her annual ground rent of 422 dollars for Nos. 14 and No. 15 Minamiyamate "under protest" because local authorities were planning to build a public road between the two properties. Continues Barff:

> In the initial plan of lot No. 14 contained in the title deed (Japanese) under which I hold the property, it is clearly shown that the lot is bounded on the south side (as to its upper

---

[72] *List of Foreign Residents of the Nagasaki Foreign Settlement*, Vol.3), 2??. The name Thorton Clayton does not appear in any subsequent documents.
[73] Measor later held an auction of household furniture at "No. 14C" Minamiyamate, obviously not the former Alt House.
[74] *The Nagasaki Press*, November 16, 1900

portion) by No. 15, thus clearly proving that no right of way between the two lots was claimed by the authorities at the time the original title deed was granted. Under these circumstances, I formally protest against the separating of the two lots by a public road unless adequate compensation is made to me.[75]

The letter was obviously penned by some other person in a neat script, with a space left for Barff's signature at the bottom. Moreover, the sender's address is given as "No. 14 Cliff Field." If not an error, this indicates that Kate Barff was using the name Cliff Field, not only to designate No. 15 Minamiyamate, but as a general appellation for her extensive Minamiyamate properties including No. 14 Minamiyamate. The outcome of Barff's protest is unclear, but Nagasaki authorities went ahead with the construction of public roads on the hillside—to such an extent that it is difficult today to discern the original features of the neighborhood.

In February 1903, now living in her original house at No. 15 Minamiyamate, Kate Barff sold No. 14 Minamiyamate to the influential British merchant and longtime Nagasaki resident Frederick Ringer and his wife Carolina. By now, the iconic stone bungalow was already one of the oldest and most romantic buildings in the former Nagasaki Foreign Settlement, tinted deeply in the deposits of history and perched on the hillside overlooking Nagasaki Harbor, watching the dramatic changes unfolding in Japan's relationship with the outside world.

Kate Barff died in 1922 at the Kaida Hotel on Sagarimatsu Creek, aged eighty-nine years and one of the longest and oldest foreign residents of Nagasaki. She was buried with her husband at Sakamoto International Cemetery, where her gravestone can still be seen today.

---

[75] Kate Barff to Y. Harakawa [sic], September 21, 1901 (*Raikan*, 1901)

Chapter 4
The Ringer Dynasty

J apan's victory in the Sino-Japanese War of 1894-95 caused a sharp boost in Nagasaki's fortunes as the closest port to China. In March 1896, seven Russian warships arrived for rest and replenishment, and the American naval presence showed a similar increase after the Spanish-American War and the cession of the Philippines to the United States. The vessels of international shipping companies also made Nagasaki a port-of-call and pulled the city headlong into the commercial hubbub of East Asia. In an 1896 report, Nagasaki British consul Joseph H. Longford expresses optimism about the future of the port as follows:

> Nagasaki is, of all Eastern ports, perhaps that which is most frequented by foreign men-of-war of all nationalities, and it would not be an excessive estimate to say that fully $1,000,000 are annually spent in the port by their crews and on the purchase of supplies, a great portion of which goes into Japanese hands, directly or indirectly. Large sums are also disbursed by mail and other merchant steamers for supplies, and by tourists and other temporary residents, especially by Russians, large numbers of whom from Vladivostok are now making the port a winter residence. But in addition to Nagasaki there are other ports which furnish an outlet for the productions of Southern Japan, the principal being Shimonoseki, Moji, and Kuchinotsu, and all three may be considered as subsidiary ports to Nagasaki... With the single exception of the French, all lines of mail steamers now running to the East call at Nagasaki both on their outward and inward voyages, and this is

the only port of call either in China or Japan of the magnificent vessels of the Russian Volunteer Fleet.[76]

The most important foreign business enterprise in Nagasaki and Shimonoseki was Holme, Ringer & Co. headed by a native of Norwich, England and former Glover & Co. tea inspector named Frederick Ringer. While other foreign residents like Thomas B. Glover, William J. Alt and Henry J. Hunt had left for greener pastures in Kobe and Yokohama, Ringer had remained in Nagasaki and made the city a permanent home. In 1897, in addition to the import/export business and a long list of insurance and banking agencies, Holme, Ringer & Co. represented twenty different international steamship companies, fully five times more than the runner-up Browne & Co.[77]

Every time a foreign steamship called at Nagasaki, the Holme, Ringer & Co. staff arranged for inspections by customs officials and insurance company representatives, supervised the loading and unloading of cargo and mail, assisted foreign travelers with immigration and emigration procedures, and commissioned all the tasks related to conveyance aboard of coal, water and foodstuffs. The boom enjoyed by Nagasaki is reflected by trade statistics: the total import trade, which included items such as kerosene, foodstuffs, cotton cloth, dyes and paints, locomotives, machinery and metals, shot from 3.5 million yen in 1893 to 19 million yen in 1898.[78]

One of the projects initiated by Frederick Ringer in the heat of Nagasaki's prosperity was the Nagasaki Hotel. Designed by British architect Josiah Conder, the three-story brick building featured an elaborate wooden façade with balconies overlooking the harbor, finely appointed interiors, dining facilities for 120 guests, private telephones in each guest room, and its own electric power plant. Frederick Ringer served as general manager of the joint-stock company established to run the hotel. When it opened in September 1898, it was hailed as the finest Western-style hotel in the Far East.

Various other factors were contributing to Nagasaki's day in the sun. The construction of the Kyūshū Railway had reached

---

⁷⁶ "Report on the Trade and Navigation of Nagasaki for 1896," quoted in full in *The Nagasaki Press*, December, 8 and 9, 1897
⁷⁷ *The Chronicle and Directory for China and Japan*, 1897 issue
⁷⁸ Nagasaki City Chronology, 128-33

completion the same year, absorbing the once isolated town into the network of overland transportation stretching to the urban centers of Osaka and Tokyo. Foreign travelers were arriving by the thousands, spilling money in souvenir shops, bars and hotels in the labyrinth of old streets, and the Mitsubishi Nagasaki Shipyard was producing steamships granted Class-A status by Lloyd's inspectors. The mood of optimism was such that the revision of international treaties and abolition of extraterritoriality in July 1899 passed all but unnoticed.

The Nagasaki Hotel symbolized Nagasaki's prosperity as an international port, commanding a panoramic view of the harbor from its narrow waterfront perch. (Private Collection)

The Ringer Family

In 1883, Frederick Ringer married Carolina Rosina Pye (nee Gower) in Nagasaki. Born in Italy, Carolina was the daughter of British civil engineer Erasmus H.M. Gower, who had come to Nagasaki in 1876 to supervise operations at the Takashima Colliery. Carolina married Edmund Pye, a leading foreign resident of Amoy, China, but her husband died of a sudden illness, and she retreated to Nagasaki to

93

join her father. She met Frederick in the social rounds of the small foreign community while living in the Western-style house at No. 27B Minamiyamate.[79]

Frederick and Carolina were the parents of three children: Frederick (Freddie), Lina and Sydney born in 1884, 1886 and 1891, respectively. The family lived at No. 2 Minamiyamate, the hillside lot between the Glover house at No. 3 Minamiyamate and No. 14 Minamiyamate. Referred to affectionately as *Niban* (Number Two) by the family, the house, built like the other two houses by master carpenter Koyama Hidenoshin, was a similar but smaller version of No. 14 Minamiyamate, featuring walls and veranda columns of Amakusa sandstone and chimneys protruding from a Japanese-style roof, with windows commanding a view over Nagasaki Harbor, the Mitsubishi Nagasaki Shipyard sprawling along the opposite shore, and the green-clad islands dotting the mouth of the harbor in the distance.

Frederick and Carolina Ringer and their children lived in purely English style, assisted by a team of faithful servants inhabiting adjacent quarters. The servants prepared European meals, tended the children according to Carolina's instructions, cleaned furniture and polished silver, and kept the imported rose vines and begonia bushes carefully trimmed. It was almost as though a small British estate had been transplanted onto the Nagasaki hillside, with a change of staff and the introduction of a few exotic utensils and works of art, but with customs, manners and everything else intact.

The two Ringer sons, Freddie and Sydney, were shuttled off to boarding schools in Britain, the former attending Edinburgh Academy, the alma mater of *Treasure Island* author Robert Louis Stevenson, and the latter St. Paul's School, one of the first nine public schools in England originally attached to St. Paul's Cathedral in London. But it went without saying that they would return to Nagasaki and line up behind their father in the company business. When he acquired No. 14 Minamiyamate in February 1903, Frederick Ringer was obviously envisioning the house as a residence for his sons after they returned to their hometown.

---

[79] For further information about the life and times of the Ringer family, see: Brian Burke-Gaffney, *Holme, Ringer & Co.: The Rise and Fall of a British Enterprise in Japan, 1868-1940* (Brill, 2013)

94

Frederick **Ringer** later in life.
(Below) Carolina Ringer with her
three children: left to right, Sydney,
Frederick (Freddie) and Lina.
(Private Collection)

The Russo-Japanese War of 1904-05 cast a pall over Ringer's optimism by curtailing the visits of foreign ships and irreversibly changing the city's economic underpinnings. One of the first casualties was the Nagasaki Hotel. The company running the hotel declared bankruptcy in 1904 and sputtered along over the following months under the direct management of Holme, Ringer & Co.

Saddened by the failure of his beloved hotel and suffering from heart disease, Frederick Ringer withdrew from the front lines of business and society. Before leaving on a trip back to England in the autumn of 1907, he visited Yokohama and signed a last will and testament itemizing the distribution of money, assets, real estate and personal belongings among his family and employees.[80] With regard to "residential property," defined as No. 2 and No. 14 Minamiyamate, he states: "I give, bequeath and devise to my wife, Carolina Rosina Ringer, absolutely and for her own use, all of the lots of land and other properties and effects included in the above classification as 'My Residential Property'."

When Frederick Ringer arrived at the Royal Hotel in his hometown of Norwich, England and wrote the words Nagasaki, Japan in the address column of the guest register, he was already in a precarious state of health. The sixty-nine-year-old veteran of trade in East Asia died in the arms of his wife Carolina and sixteen-year-old son Sydney and was buried according to his wishes beside his mother and father in Rosary Cemetery. The epitaph on the gravestone reads: "Sacred to the Memory of Frederick Ringer of Nagasaki Japan."

The Second Generation

Frederick Ringer's sons Freddie and Sydney returned to Japan in 1905 and 1909, respectively, and took up the reins of Holme, Ringer & Co., first as assistants in the company offices in Nagasaki and Shimonoseki and later as partners. In the course of their business activities and social life, the Ringer brothers, like other European men living in Japan, had many more opportunities to associate with Japanese women than with foreign women. However, their father Frederick had laid out a nonverbal ban against international marriage, probably because of the many failed relationships he had witnessed since arriving in Japan in the pre-Meiji years. As a result, the brothers and other Holme Ringer & Co. employees invariably married British women through the introduction of older staff members.

In April 1913, Sydney married Aileen Moore, the niece of company colleague Percy J. Buckland. The ceremony at the English

---

[80] "The Estate of Frederick Ringer," dated September 18, 1907 (FO 917/1561)

96

Church in Higashiyamate was attended by a large group of friends and colleagues. The Japanese guests included the governor of Nagasaki Prefecture and his wife, the mayor of Nagasaki City, and leaders of business and industry. The grand reception held later at the Buckland residence in Minamiyamate reflected the goodwill of the multinational community and the high standing of Holme, Ringer & Co. in the city.

Group photograph (section) from the wedding reception of Sydney and Aileen Ringer in April 1913. (Seated left to right) Mrs. Rinoie, Sydney, Aileen, Rinoie Ryūsuke (Nagasaki Prefecture Governor), Carolina, Neil B. Reid (Holme, Ringer & Co. executive) and Lina. Freddie is standing behind the bride. (Courtesy of Saitō Yoshirō)

Freddie followed Sydney in November, marrying Buckland's sister Alcidie Eva Buckland in a ceremony at Christ Church in Wanstead, London. The couple returned to Nagasaki in March the following year and went directly to No. 14 Minamiyamate, where

Carolina Ringer was waiting to celebrate the beginning of a new chapter in the saga of the Ringer family. The writer of an article in the local English-language newspaper described the event as follows:

> On Saturday evening Mrs. Ringer was 'At Home' at her residence, 14, Minamiyamate, giving a large circle of friends an opportunity to welcome her elder son Mr. F.E.E. Ringer, and his bride (Miss Alcidie E. Buckland) back to Nagasaki. The marriage took place in England in November and Mr. and Mrs. Ringer arrived here a few days ago. After the reception of the guests, dancing began and was continued until a late hour. Many beautiful wedding presents from friends in England and the Far East were on display.[81]

From that time onward, the stretch of hillside encompassing the two colonial-style stone bungalows at No. 2 and No. 14 Minami-yamate became the exclusive domain of the Ringer family and the homes of Freddie and Sydney and their families, all under the watch of *grand dame* Carolina Rosina Ringer.

Frederick and Carolina's daughter Lina Jessie Ringer also returned to her hometown after schooling in England and moved in with her mother at No. 14 Minamiyamate. In 1907, she ignored her father's protests and eloped with Willmott H. Lewis, the dashing Welsh-born former editor of *The Nagasaki Press* now gaining fame for his work as a freelance journalist. The couple took up residence in Yokohama, where Lina gave birth to a daughter the following year. In 1910, Willmott accepted an invitation to serve as editor at *The Manila Times*, and Lina gave birth to a second daughter in the Philippines. In 1916, however, Willmott and Lina separated, the former drifting to Europe and the latter returning to Nagasaki to live with her mother. By the following year, Willmott was working for *The New York World*, writing erudite commentary on political affairs in the Far East that found its way onto the pages of newspapers worldwide. It probably also caught the attention of Lina, sitting reading *The Nagasaki Press* in a sunlit room at No. 14 Minamiyamate and waiting patiently with her daughters for the Welshman's return.

---

[81] *The Nagasaki Press*, March 17, 1914.

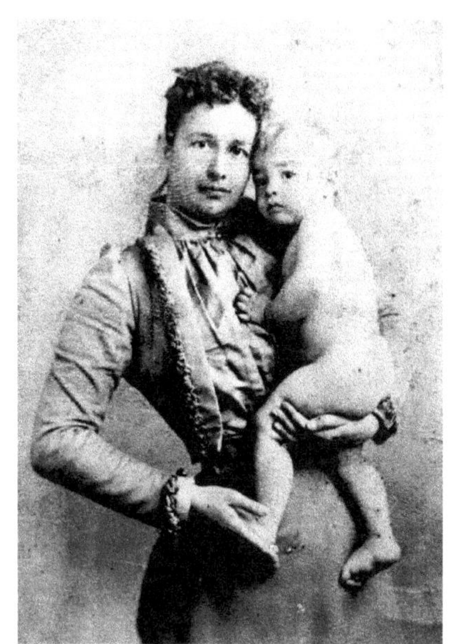

Lina Jessie Lewis (nee Ringer)
with her daughter circa 1910.
(Courtesy of Elizabeth Newton)

The Garden Fete

Alcidie Ringer's brother Percy J. Buckland and the other employees who had supervised the affairs of Holme, Ringer & Co. in the wake of Frederick Ringer's death submitted their resignations and transferred control of the family business to the two Ringer brothers. Freddie and Sydney filled the spaces vacated by their mentors, taking the lead in business activities, participating in the official round of parties and commemorative events, and serving as acting consuls for Norway, Sweden, Belgium and other countries in the ports of Nagasaki and Shimonoseki. Freddie's wife Alcidie gave birth to a daughter, named Alcidie Jennie Ringer, in August 1914. Sydney and Aileen Ringer also became the parents of two sons, Michael and Vanya. The addition of Lina's daughters brought the total number of Ringer grandchildren to five, all living in the two family houses on the Minamiyamate hillside.

The outbreak of World War I exerted a positive effect on Nagasaki in that the number of ships visiting the port increased, sparking a commensurate leap in business activity and an unprecedented boom for the local shipbuilding and munitions industries led by Mitsubishi. British residents remained mostly exempt from conscription and other war-related hardships, but, like their counterparts in Shanghai and Yokohama, they formed local branches of the Patriotic League of Britons Overseas and British Ladies Patriotic League and contributed eagerly to war-related charities. All of the activities conducted by British residents won sympathy and cooperation from Japanese citizens and reinforced their mutual sense of solidarity as allies in the war.

To date, except for short stints as a school and U. S. Consulate, the house at No. 14 Minamiyamate had been a secluded villa enjoyed only by family members and a few special guests. However, the opulent house and garden came to life on May 20, 1916 when Carolina Ringer threw open the property for an event advertised in newspapers as the "Garden Fete."

Planned by Carolina and her British compatriots as a way to raise funds for the maintenance of Red Cross hospital beds in Europe, the party saw the participation of a large number of British residents, friendly neutrals and Japanese friends including political and business leaders. The author of a long report in the local English-language newspaper described the setting as follows:

> The fete was held in the well-kept grounds of Mrs. Ringer's residence, 14, Minamiyamate, which commands a splendid view of the harbor, and the Japanese visitors were especially impressed with the beauty of their surroundings. The veranda of the house made a fine platform for the concert entertainers, and shades were erected in front for the audience and tea. Bunting had been kindly lent by the City Office and bluejackets from the Italian gunboat *Sebastiano Caboto* spent many hours in putting it up in marquee form and decorating with flags and lanterns. The result was extremely serviceable and pretty. In other parts of the grounds were stalls and other devices for alluring money and all were well patronized throughout the afternoon.[82]

Tickets were available at one yen for adults and twenty-five sen for children. The latter charge also applied to the amah (nurse-

---

[82] *The Nagasaki Press*, May 23, 1916

maids) attending to children. The organizers served refreshments and sweets at booths set up in the garden and sold everything from handmade doilies to flags, toys and potted plants. One of the highlights was "Bran Pie," a game in which gifts were hidden in a tub full of bran and pulled out at random, winning both money and laughter from participants. A traditional game of "Coconut Shy" (throwing wooden balls at a row of coconuts balanced on posts) was also set up in one of the stalls. An orchestra comprised of local musicians, both foreign and Japanese, entertained the guests from the stone-paved veranda stretching along the façade. Carolina Ringer joined as pianist and her daughter Lina as a singer.

The veranda also saw presentations of the Pigeon Walk, Fox Trot and other popular dances, all to the delight of the audience. The music ended with a solo piano performance of the British and Japanese national anthems by Carolina Ringer, concluding "one of the happiest social events of the foreign community of Nagasaki." When the tallies came in, the event was found to have earned more that 1,250 yen, enough to maintain two and a half hospital beds for a year. The significance of the sum is indicated by the fact that, only the previous year, Robert Walker had purchased the large house and garden at No. 28 Minamiyamate for 1,300 yen.

Japanese guests relax at one of Carolina Ringer's parties in front of the house at No. 14 Minamiyamate. (Courtesy of Ueda Katsuko)

The Garden Fete of May 1916 was the first in a series of social and charitable parties held at No. 14 Minamiyamate, hosted by Carolina Ringer and attended by guests from the multinational community of Nagasaki. The success of the events prompted Ringer and her lady friends to organize a similar Garden Fete in May 1917, which attracted an even greater number of participants including the governor of Nagasaki Prefecture, mayor of Nagasaki City and their wives. Then in November the same year, No. 14 Minamiyamate opened its gates for a bazaar held to assist refugees of the Russian Revolution passing through Nagasaki in distress. While Carolina Ringer supervised the musical entertainment, Lina dressed up as Madame de Pompadour and told fortunes, collecting thanks from the Russian consul in Nagasaki as well as donations from guests.

By the following year, however, the spirit of charity and conviviality was waning in tandem with global fatigue over the war dragging on in Europe. The Garden Fete planned for Saturday May 4, 1918 had to be postponed to the following Monday due to rain, and illness prevented both Carolina and Lina from participating.

Carolina Rosina Ringer (left) with her daughter Lina in Nagasaki. (Private Collection)

Grand dame of the foreign community and an accomplished pianist, Carolina Ringer (right) poses with a friend in front of the stairs of her opulent house, probably during one of the parties she held at No. 14 Minamiyamate. She spent more than forty years in Nagasaki before her trip to Europe in 1921. (Private collection)

Carolina Rosina Ringer's signature (from a certificate
in the registers at Ōura Catholic Church,
where she was a parishioner)

Death of Carolina Ringer

Despite Lina Lewis's hopes for a return to family life, journalistic achievements took her husband Willmott in the opposite direction. In 1920, he assumed the prestigious position of correspondent for *The Times* of London and moved to Washington DC, abandoning his family and giving truth to his late father-in-law's darkest predictions.

Lina continued to live with her mother, older brother and sister-in-law in the house at No. 14 Minamiyamate, participating occasionally in social events but mostly hiding from the outside world. When they reached school age, her two daughters attended the Sacred Heart School (Seishin Jogakkō) run by French Catholic nuns at No. 16 Minamiyamate, only a short walk from the house. The Ringer family members were associated nominally with the Church of England, but both girls would convert to the Catholic religion in adulthood, probably as a result of their education in Nagasaki or the influence of their grandmother Carolina, who was also Catholic.

In July 1922, Lina departed Nagasaki for England, leaving her daughters in the care of her brother Sydney. Her absence from her hometown would turn out to be permanent, but the only inkling is a short article in *The Nagasaki Press* stating that her friends in the music department at Kwassui Girls School held a farewell gathering in her honor. Lina probably wanted to join her mother Carolina, who had also left Japan by the time and traveled with a friend to enjoy a vacation in Europe.

Lina's journey abroad may have also been motivated by a desire, or rather a last desperate attempt, to restore her relationship with Willmott Lewis. In any case, she lingered far longer than expected in the country of her ancestors. In June 1924, Sydney, his wife Aileen and two sons accompanied Lina's daughters on a voyage to England and delivered the two girls safely into the arms of their mother. Carolina, who had spent the summer in Italy, traveled to London to meet her children and grandchildren. The family was still enjoying a reunion when Carolina came down with a sudden illness. She died in London in September the same year, bringing an end to a colorful life of sixty-seven years, much of it spent in her second hometown of Nagasaki. The entry in the *England & Wales National Probate Calendar* (Index of Wills and Administrations) gives her address as "14 Minami Yamate Nagasaki Japan."

In March 1925, Lina filed a petition for divorce in the British High Court of Justice, charging her husband with three counts of adultery between 1920 and 1925 with "a woman unknown to your Petitioner."[83] The judge hearing the case approved the divorce and ordered Willmott H. Lewis to pay a substantial alimony, but the famous journalist was quickly relieved of the greater part of the burden: Lina died in Epsom, Surrey in 1929 at the age of forty-three, her early demise attributed to a broken heart by her descendants.

A Beautiful European Residence

In 1919, the Globe Encyclopedia Company of Chicago published a 931-page leather-bound book entitled *Present-Day Impressions of Japan*, probably the first of its kind to provide detailed information on the history, culture and businesses of almost every major city in the country, along with hundreds of photographs depicting people, buildings and scenery. The section on Nagasaki focuses on Holme, Ringer & Co. as the leading business entity in the port:

> To the traveller and merchant of the Far East the name of Holme, Ringer is almost synonymous for that of the port, so intimately associated is its history with Nagasaki. The firm will celebrate its fiftieth anniversary on November 2nd of this year (1918), and has, therefore, the unique record of being the sole representative of foreign trade in this centre for half a century, during which period it has been connected with the various progressive commercial and industrial movements to a most interesting degree, and, indeed, is responsible for the inception of many... Messrs. Holme, Ringer are large holders of both business and residential property in Nagasaki and it may be added that the firm is the centre of those organizations which have given this small community so honorable a position amongst the supporters of war charities.[84]

The photographs of Nagasaki include a shot of the Holme, Ringer & Co. office on the Ōura waterfront and also a photograph of

---

[83] 'L.J. Lewis vs. W.H. Lewis' (National Archives of the UK, J 77/2167)
[84] W.H. Morton-Cameron (ed.), *Present-Day Impressions of Japan* (Chicago: The Globe Encyclopedia Company, 1919), 808-9

the house at No. 14 Minamiyamate taken with a wide-angle lens. Entitled "A beautiful European residence at Nagasaki," the latter reflects the status of the building as the most prominent and iconic residence in the former Nagasaki Foreign Settlement and a symbol of the city's colorful history of international and cultural exchange.

A rare wide-angle photograph of the house at No. 14 Minamiyamate was featured in *Present-Day Impressions of Japan*, published in 1919. The Italianate fountain in front of the portico is evident, along with a large number of potted plants placed along the garden path.

Miura Tamaki in Nagasaki

The stone bungalow at No. 14 Minamiyamate came to public attention again in June 1922 when *prima donna* Miura Tamaki visited Nagasaki with her Italian accompanist Aldo Franchetti to give a recital at a local theater. Although still relatively unknown in her native Japan, Miura had gained fame in Europe and North America for her portrayal of the tragic heroine in the opera *Madame Butterfly*.

The morning before the recital, Miura and Franchetti, both visiting Nagasaki for the first time, asked Nagasaki scholar Mutō Chōzō to show them sites connected with the opera. Mutō suggested No. 14 Minamiyamate, which had served as the U. S. Consulate from 1893 to 1898, a period coinciding with the publication of the novelette *Madame Butterfly* in New York. In the original story by John Luther Long, Cho-Cho-san (Butterfly) makes love with

Lieutenant Pinkerton and then, after his departure and the birth of their son, waits for three years believing that the lieutenant will return as promised. The narrative reaches a climax when she sees Pinkerton's warship enter Nagasaki Harbor and rushes to the U. S. Consulate seeking information, only to meet Pinkerton's American wife and later commit suicide in despair.[85]

By a remarkable coincidence, the Nagasaki U. S. Consul at the time of Miura's visit was I.C. Correll, who had been born in Nagasaki during the family sojourn in the 1890s. The consul's mother Jennie Correll, sister of John Luther Long, was also in Nagasaki, visiting from Tokyo. Mutō Chōzō introduced the Americans to Miura and Franchetti and guided the group on an excursion to the Minamiyamate hillside to see the fabled house:

> On Friday morning Madame Miura, Mrs. Correll, and Mr. and Mrs. I.C. Correll, accompanied by Professor Muto, paid a visit to 14, Minami-yamate, the residence of Mrs. Ringer, which was formerly the residence of the United States Consuls at Nagasaki and figures largely in the pathetic story of 'Madame Butterfly.' Photographs were taken which will be very interesting souvenirs of the opera and Madame Miura's visit to Nagasaki.

The English-language newspaper hailed Miura as "Madame Butterfly at Nagasaki," but the prima donna sang only two pieces from the opera and devoted most of her recital to popular Japanese songs, much better appreciated by the Japanese audience. The author of the newspaper article noted that: "Madame Miura wore a European dress during the first half of the Programme, but after the interval she changed into her native costume, so that she fully looked the part of 'Butterfly.'" During the intermission, Aldo Franchetti addressed the audience with the help of Mutō Chōzō, expressing thanks for the enthusiastic response and pointing out that:

> 'Madame Butterfly,' the opera in which Madame Miura has made a name in Europe, America, and other parts of the world, belongs essentially to Nagasaki, the story being woven around

---

85 For further information see: Brian Burke-Gaffney, *Starcrossed: A Biography of Madame Butterfly* (Eastbridge, 2004)

the port and the scenery taken from 14, Minami Yamate. The story was written by an uncle of the present American consul of Nagasaki, Mr. Correll. It was later put to music by Giacomo Puccini.[86]

(Left to right) Mutō Chōzō, Aldo Franchetti, Miura Tamaki and Jennie Correll pose for a photograph in front of the fountain at No. 14 Minamiyamate. The woman in the rear is probably U. S. Consul I.C. Correll's wife. (Glover Garden)

John Luther Long and Giacomo Puccini borrowed heavily from French author Pierre Loti's travelogue *Madame Chrysanthéme* in the creation of the novelette and opera *Madame Butterfly*. But Loti lived in a Japanese neighborhood during his visit to Nagasaki in 1885 and, in fact, wrote disparagingly of the nondescript Western-style facilities he saw on the waterfront and hillsides: "Where are we in reality? In the United States? In some English colony in Australia, or in New Zealand? Consular residences, custom-house offices, manufactories; a dry dock in which a Russian frigate was lying; on the heights

------

[86] "Madame Butterfly at Nagasaki," *The Nagasaki Press*, June 4, 1922

108

the large European concession, sprinkled with villas, and on the quays, American bars for the sailors."[87]

Aldo Franchetti, by contrast, was enamored of No. 14 Minamiyamate, a house that perhaps reminded him, not just of the tale of a heartbroken girl, but also the long journey of European colonial expansion in East Asia and all the romantic episodes that unfolded along the way. Four years later, he would write his own musical tragedy, an operetta in one act entitled *Namiko-San* unveiled in Chicago with Miura Tamaki playing the leading role.

Gin and Dynamite

After the death of their mother in 1924, Freddie and Sydney Ringer settled into a quiet life in Nagasaki, living comfortably in the historic houses at No. 14 and No. 2 Minamiyamate, respectively. Twelve years old at the time of her grandmother's death, Freddie's only daughter Alcidie Jennie Ringer, who had spent her early childhood in Nagasaki, left Japan for studies at a boarding school in England.

Alcidie Jennie Ringer as a child with Obama Yoshi, who served the Ringer family for many years as a maid and amah. Nagasaki Harbor is visible in the background. (Private collection)

---

[87] Pierre Loti, *Madame Chrysanthéme* (Paris: Edouard Guillaume et Cie., 1893) (From the 1920 English translation by Laura Ensor)

Freddie (left) and Sydney Ringer took over operation of Holme, Ringer & Co. but faced an economic downturn in their hometown. (Private collection)

Freddie and Sydney Ringer kept Holme, Ringer & Co. running amid a relentless decline in Nagasaki's activity as an international trade port. Fewer foreign merchantmen and passenger liners than ever were calling, even to take on the bunker coal so prized at the end of the previous century. In 1925, only ninety-four foreign merchantmen entered Nagasaki Harbor, less than 13% of the peak figure of 726 ships recorded in 1898. The population of the former foreign settlement dwindled year by year as shipyards, coal mines and munitions factories usurped the importance of import and export businesses in the city economy.

The Nagasaki Hotel had closed in 1908, soon after Frederick Ringer's death in England. A Japanese merchant named Mori Arayoshi revived the establishment, but it faltered again in 1924 and the buiding was torn down. Although not as much as a foundation stone remains today, the hotel silverware was discovered recently at the Nara Hotel, which luckily shared the engraved initials NH.[88] Other Western-style hotels such as the Belle Vue Hotel and Cliff House also

---

[88] Burke-Gaffney, *Holme, Ringer & Company*, 99

closed, never to reopen, and the English-language newspaper *The Nagasaki Press*, the voice of the foreign community, fell silent in the summer of 1928. The Ringer brothers took turns enjoying yearlong holidays in England, leaving the daily drudgery to the remaining brother and a few faithful British and Japanese employees. Freddie's wife Alcidie joked that the company name should be changed to "Home Ringer" because one of the brothers was always home on leave.

The house at No. 14 Minamiyamate continued its career as the most majestic private residence in Nagasaki but witnessed none of the grand public celebrations convened by Carolina Ringer in previous years. Now only a few privileged guests ascended the path up the hillside and enjoyed the hospitality of Freddie and Alcidie in their palatial bungalow. One was twenty-four-year-old Prince George, son of King George V, who visited Nagasaki on an unofficial visit in November 1926, spent a day hiking to the seaside village of Mogi, then dined with the Ringer family and a few other British residents at No. 14 Minamiyamate. Another was a British friend named Arnold Graham who arrived in Nagasaki in 1931 during a sailing expedition to East Asia and visited the Ringer house, where, he later reported, "Freddie poured gin liberally down our salty throats."

The same year that Freddie and his seafaring friends guzzled gin on the veranda at No. 14 Minamiyamate, Japanese military personnel denotated dynamite charges near the Japan-owned South Manchuria Railway near Mukden (Shenyang), initiating a series of events that led to the occupation of Manchuria by Japanese troops, the establishment of the puppet state of Manchukuo and, when the United States and Britain protested, Japan's diplomatic isolation and withdrawal from the League of Nations.

In the early 1930s, perhaps sensing the increasingly tenuous position of foreigners in Japan, Freddie and Alcidie Ringer hired a professional photographer to record scenes of the interior, exterior and gardens of the family house at No. 14 Minamiyamate. Preserved today by family descendants, the forty photographs provide an invaluable record of the historic building—the former Alt House and U. S. Consulate preserved today as a National Important Cultural Property—as well as an intimate look into the lifestyles of foreign residents prior to the calamity of World War II. The following pages present a few excerpts from the album.

(Above) Freddie and Alcidie pose with their dogs on the lawn in front of No. 14 Minamiyamate. (Below) The portico and front steps, with the pool around the Italianate fountain on the right.

(Above) View of the front garden and entrance to No. 14 Minamiyamate, looking north. (Below) Part of the veranda has been converted into a sunroom and the space to the side into a car park. The wisteria tree is in full bloom, reaching up over the trellis.

(Above) A greenhouse has been constructed at the southern end of the veranda. Potted plants are placed on the veranda once used as seating for parties and a stage for musical presentations. (Below) The entrance vestibule is decorated with plants, carpets and wall hangings; the carpeted interior corridor is also scattered with plants and furnishings. (Appendix: Rooms 1, 2 and 3).

The parlor and dining room feature ornate furniture and coal-burning fireplaces. The various trappings of the house went unaccounted for after World War II. (Appendix: Rooms 5 and 10).

The spacious living room captured from the north (above) and looking from the door. The room is decorated with Japanese as well as European furnishings, such as the folding screen visible on the left (below). Light floods inside from the tall windows along the front and side of the building. (Appendix: Room 4).

The master bedroom (above) and the small bedroom at the southern end of the house, with the fireplace installed diagonally in the latter. (Appendix: Rooms 6 and 17).

The sprawling property had a private driveway, reconstructed in recent decades as a public road. The greenhouse no longer exists.

Above the Cultural Divide

Freddie and Alcidie Ringer's only daughter Alcidie Jennie Ringer returned from boarding school in England in 1932 at the age of eighteen and joined her parents at No. 14 Minamiyamate. Over the following months, she participated in the round of social events in her hometown and also pursued her interest in Japanese art, a subject which had apparently fascinated her since childhood. Her deft painting of a Japanese woman in a kimono executed on a *kakemono* scroll is preserved today in Nagasaki and still bears the red seal showing the initials AJR and a handwritten signature using the Chinese characters 林賀, literally "forest felicitation" but pronounced *ringa*, thus simulating Ringer. She also devoted herself to the esoteric art of *bonkei*, or "scenery on a tray" and gained such expertise that her Japanese teacher granted her a license to teach along with the *gagō* (professional name) Keichō. The certificate, donated to Nagasaki City by Alcidie's family, is also preserved at Glover Garden.

118

(Above) Ringer family members pose with friends on the lawn at No. 14 Minamiyamate. (Standing left to right, every other person) Alcidie Jennie, Freddie, Alcidie, Kuraba Tomisaburō (son of Thomas B. Glover) and Aileen. Sydney is sitting on the lawn far left. (Below) Painting in Japanese style by Alcidie Jennie Ringer. Alcidie's interest in Japanese art signaled a lowering of the cultural fence between the foreign and Japanese communities.

In October 1936, at the age of twenty-two, Alcidie married Folmer Bjergfelt, a Danish engineer and employee of the Great Northern Telegraph Company. The couple later moved to Yokohama, where Alcidie gave birth to two sons. Folmer meanwhile had to fend off increasingly heated demands from the Japanese government for the transfer of rights to the submarine telegraph cables controlled by the Danish company.

(Left to right), unknown, Vanya, Freddie, Michael and Sydney pose at the front door of No. 14 Minamiyamate in formal attire, apparently celebrating some occasion. (Private collection)

Sydney and Aileen Ringer's sons Michael and Vanya—heirs to the family business in Nagasaki and Shimonoseki—studied in England and, like their cousin Alcidie, returned to Nagasaki in the early 1930s to begin a new career as adults in their hometown. Youthful and exuberant, the two brothers brought a breath of fresh air to the dusty former Nagasaki Foreign Settlement, not to mention hope for an upturn in the fortunes of Holme, Ringer & Co. They also enjoyed a modicum of celebrity status in the Japanese community. Tomita Sumiko, daughter-in-law of Ringer family gardener Tomita Ikutarō, relates that girls in the neighborhood almost swooned every time Michael or Vanya passed nearby wearing suits and silk hats of the latest fashion. Photographs capture them posing with Japanese friends and fellow Nagasaki Club members (among whom they are conspicuously youthful) and frolicking at costume balls and parties in Japanese restaurants. Born and raised after the abolition of extraterritoriality, the Ringer brothers and their cousin Alcidie were attune to Japanese culture and able to transcend the barriers that once separated the foreign and Japanese communities.

The Silver Jubilee

The Silver Jubilee celebrated on May 6, 1935 marked twenty-five years of George V as the King of the United Kingdom and the British Dominions, and Emperor of India. The event was marked with large-scale events in London and other places with British connections around the world. It was the first in history to celebrate the Silver Jubilee of a British monarch. The Ringer family and other British residents of Nagasaki celebrated the occasion, first with a service at the Holy Trinity Church in Ōmura-machi made available by Nippon Seikōkai (the Japanese arm of the Church of England) and later a garden party at No. 14 Minamiyamate. The organizers had to bring the events forward to May 5, the day before the actual anniversary, because all the local clergymen were required to attend a general synod in Sendai. As a result, the Nagasaki celebration was hailed as the first in the British Empire.

Freddie and Alcidie Ringer hosted the garden party, probably looking back nostalgically on the fundraising galas convened by Carolina Ringer during World War I. Blessed with fine weather, the party was attended by leading members of both the Japanese and foreign communities who took seats at tables arranged along the veranda and around the Italianate fountain in the garden.

The author of a newspaper report on the party described the house at No. 14 Minamiyamate as "not only a beautiful place, but one that was especially appropriate owing to the long connection of the family with the port and the many occasions when it has been similarly used by the British community." [89]

---

[89] *The Japan Chronicle*, May 10, 1935.

(Above) The garden party held in front of the Ringer house at No. 14 Minamiyamate in May 1935 was attended by a large number of Japanese and foreign guests. Kuraba Tomisaburō is standing in the center speaking to friends. (Below) Sydney Ringer (seated second from right) and British friends sit on the stairs, with the jubilee flag raised behind. (Private collection)

Launching of the *Musashi*

The smiles and happy conversation at the garden party contrasted sharply with Japan's deteriorating international relationships and the rising specter of militarism and xenophobia. In July 1937, Japanese and Chinese forces exchanged fire at Marco Polo Bridge near Beijing, and the Imperial Japanese Army launched its controversial project of aggression on the continent. The Japanese government enacted the New Military Secrets Protection Law, which gave authorities far-reaching powers to arrest and imprison anyone suspected of collecting sensitive information or leaking military secrets, followed in March the following year by the National Mobilization Law. The latter placed Japan firmly on an arc to war by limiting freedom of speech in the media, extending government control to all civilian organizations including labor unions, and making war production the foremost priority in budget allocations.

The Imperial Japanese Navy started construction of two 70,000-ton battleships, the *Yamato* at the Imperial Japanese Navy Shipyard in Kure (Hiroshima Prefecture) and the *Musashi* at the Mitsubishi Nagasaki Shipyard. Authorities hid the building berth in Nagasaki from view behind rope curtains and rolled out a tight blanket of security to ensure that outsiders, particularly foreigners, remained unaware of the activity in the shipyard. Anything left of the peaceful and cosmopolitan port of Nagasaki disappeared into the shadow of the city's new role as a military stronghold.

The military police supervising the efforts at camouflage were vexed by the stubborn presence of the Ringer family and other foreigners enjoying a clear view of the Mitsubishi Nagasaki Shipyard from their hillside houses. As legal residents with consular credentials, Freddie and Sydney Ringer were able to brush off flak from the military police and remain in their Minamiyamate houses without fear of harassment. But a different set of circumstances affected Kuraba Tomisaburō, the Japanese-British son of Thomas B. Glover working for many years at Holme, Ringer & Co. and associating closely with both Japanese and foreign residents. In April 1939, Kuraba sold his house—the famous Ipponmatsu at No. 3 Minamiyamate—to Mitsubishi and moved to No. 9 Minamiyamate (the house initially built and inhabited by William J. Alt) with his wife Waka, abruptly ending the Glover family presence on the Minamiyamate hillside.

Freddie Ringer died in Nagasaki on February 23, 1940 at the age of fifty-five, his early demise undoubtedly aggravated by the collapse of friendly relations between Japan and Britain and the grim situation facing the family company. An article on the funeral carried in the Kobe newspaper *The Japan Chronicle* gives no indication of trouble or conflict, reporting that the Holy Trinity Church in Ōmura-machi was

> crowded with a very large attendance, representative of every section of the Japanese and foreign community, and the esteem and affection with which the later Mr Ringer was regarded was shown by the very large number of floral tributes, not only by members of the local community, but by those placed in the Church by the instructions of his many friends in Japan, China and abroad.[90]

Among the Japanese attendees were "the wife of the governor of Nagasaki Prefecture, who himself was unavoidably absent" and the mayor of Nagasaki and chief justice of the Nagasaki Court of Appeals. Also on hand were the chief of police and chief of the water police, the very men who were supervising efforts to hide the battleship *Musashi* from foreign eyes and who in a few short months would be ordering the arrest and detainment of Ringer family members. Freddie's remains were cremated and the ashes strewn according to his will, and no gravestone was erected.

By now, the foreign population of Nagasaki had shriveled to a fraction of its peak around the turn of the century. The Great Northern Telegraph Company still employed eight foreigners in Nagasaki and continued to clutch rights to the submarine telegraph cables connecting Japan with the continent, as well as a number of prime lots in the former foreign settlement. On June 1, 1940, however, the company acquiesced to an ultimatum from the Ministry of Communications and transferred all rights and property to the Japanese government. Freddie Ringer's son-in-law Folmer Bjergfelt, still living with his family in Yokohama, was among a handful of Great Northern Telegraph Company employees who stayed in Japan to wrap up the affairs of the company.

---

[90] *The Japan Chronicle*, March 2, 1940.

The buildings on the Ōura waterfront (from left to right) are the American Consulate, British Consulate, Holme, Ringer & Co. office and Europa Hotel. The large building on the hillside is Kwassui Women's School. The lower right inscription reads "Passed by Nagasaki Fortress Headquarters censors on November 22, 1934," evidence of the mounting confrontation between Japan and the countries of the West. (Private collection)

The hammer quivering over the heads of the Ringer family fell unexpectedly on Sydney's two sons. Michael and Vanya were arrested on charges of espionage and taken into custody by the military police on July 27, 1940. The brothers languished in jail for almost two months until finally being brought to trial. Both were sentenced to several months of penal servitude, with a five-year stay of execution tantamount to a deportation order. They left Nagasaki for China at the end of September and traveled to India to join the British Indian Army, Michael as an intelligence officer and Vanya as a lieutenant in the elite Punjab Regiment.

Sydney Ringer meanwhile closed the company offices and made arrangements to quit Japan. Frustrated and heartbroken, he and his wife Aileen sailed out of Nagasaki Harbor for Shanghai on October 20, 1940. Neither their departure nor the collapse of Nagasaki's oldest commercial enterprise earned a word of mention in local newspapers.

Aside from Nagasaki British Consul Ferdinand C. Greatrex, who remained at his desk like the captain of a sinking ship, the only foreigner clinging to the illusion of privilege and safety on the Minamiyamate hillside was Alcidie Eva Ringer, the now sixty-four-year-old widow of Freddie Ringer. Alcidie perhaps considered herself exempt because her son-in-law Folmer Bjergfelt, a neutral Dane, had received permission to remain in Japan as an employee of the Great Northern Telegraph Company. Or perhaps she was simply reluctant to leave her familiar surroundings at No. 14 Minamiyamate. However, on the morning of December 8, 1941—the day that Mitsubishi A6M2 Zero fighters rained bombs on Pearl Harbor—policemen knocked at her door and placed her under arrest.

Alcidie's experience—from the day of her detainment until her escape on an exchange ship from Yokohama the following year—is recorded in detail in a report compiled by Ferdinand C. Greatrex for submission to the United Nations War Crimes Commission.[91]

According to Greatrex, the police escorted Alcidie to the Umegasaki Police Station, interrogated her, and then charged her with espionage on the grounds that she had listened to radio reports from Shanghai. The police were obviously grasping at straws. The radio in question was no different from any other radio decorating homes in Nagasaki at the time. Oddly enough, they made no mention of the possibility that she had spied on the Mitsubishi Nagasaki Shipyard during the construction of the *Musashi*, even though the shipyard was plainly visible from No. 14 Minamiyamate.

Two weeks later, without anything in the way of a court hearing, Alcidie was transferred to the city prison and placed in solitary confinement. Greatrex describes the city prison as follows:

On arrival at the prison on the 20th December, under wintry conditions, Mrs Ringer was deprived of all her clothes at the entrance of her cell and left for several hours with no protection against the cold but a thin prisoner 'kimono' and a pair of quilts on the matted floor. Her clothes were returned the same day, and her own bedding was brought a day or two later, but no

---

[91] TS 26/283. Greatrex interviewed Alcidie on the voyage back to Britain and wrote the report on the basis of her recollections. The case was apparently never taken up as a war crime.

heating was ever provided and, as she was not allowed slippers in the cell, she suffered severely from chilblains. The cell was about 10 ft. by 8, equipped with very primitive toilet and washing appliances and she had to carry the receptacle out and back herself each day. The examiner, while sometimes courteous, at other times adopted the most offensive bullying tactics, such as pointing at her and shouting: 'You spy. Greatrex spy', calling her a liar and saying that in Japan liars were treated like beasts, namely thrashed. On one occasion when he was evidently about to strike her, he restrained himself when she rose and indignantly asked the interpreter whether that was a Japanese gentleman's way of treating an elderly unprotected woman.

Two weeks later, Alcidie was declared guilty of all the charges against her and ordered to pay a fine of 300 yen, but she never stood in front of a judge or learned on what authority the punishments were meted out. In April the following year, she was transferred to a school on the outskirts of Nagasaki along with Ferdinand C. Greatrex and a few missionaries, elderly men with Japanese wives, and other intrepid foreigners who had ignored the many recommendations to leave Japan.

Greatrex ends his report with a paragraph about letters written but never delivered:

Mrs Ringer was not allowed to write any letters until the 2nd February, when the prison authorities allowed her to write to 'her Consul' asking him to convey to her daughter in Yokohama a message that she was well and hoping to hear from her, etc. She was informed on 11th February that her note had been delivered to the Consul by hand (Note: Actually the note was never delivered). Later she received a letter from her daughter through Argentine Consular channels, and the reply which she wrote duly reached its destination, but two subsequent letters supposed to have been despatched were suppressed and returned to her when she left the prison. At the internment establishment she was able to exchange letters with her daughter with a maximum delay in transit of about three weeks.

On July 21, 1942, the police finally allowed Alcidie Eva Ringer to go to her house at No. 14 Minamiyamate and to prepare to leave Japan by ship from Yokohama, part of an exchange agreement between the Japanese and British governments. In her affidavit to Ferdinand C. Greatrex, she reports that "wanton pilfering" had taken place during the search of the house after her arrest. When she descended the familiar path to the Nagasaki waterfront, the old family residences at No. 14 and No. 2 Minamiyamate stood empty and incongruent in the hot sunlight, already relics of a bygone way of life and a chapter in Japanese history irrevocably terminated.

Chapter 5
Conflict and Confusion

During the first weeks of 1942, the people of Nagasaki rejoiced at the news of the fall of Hong Kong and Singapore and other advances abroad by Japanese military forces, but at home they faced increasing hardships due to air defense drills, thought control, and food shortages. The government announced the enforcement of a rationing system for salt, miso, and soy sauce, and imposed strict restrictions on dress and hairstyles. A clothing ticket system was implemented, with city dwellers receiving 100 points a year and country folk eighty points that had to be used when purchasing apparel. In addition, the government ordered the reduction of newspapers throughout Japan to one per prefecture, forcing several newspapers in Nagasaki Prefecture to merge or cease publication. By now, foreign trade and the openness and modernism characteristic of Nagasaki were a thing of the past.

In the wake of the outbreak of war, the Japanese government imposed a series of legal measures to seize and dispose of enemy property, first the Enemy Property Administration Act of December 23, 1941 and then Imperial Ordinance No. 272 in late March 1942. The latter converted all the perpetual leases remaining in the former foreign settlements to ownership rights, paving the way for the unilateral sale of foreign-held land and possessions as enemy property. The impact could not have been felt any greater than by the Ringer family, who owned some seventeen lots in the former foreign settlement including the houses at No. 2, 4 and 14 Minamiyamate, the Holme, Ringer & Co. office at No. 7 Ōura, and the Nagasaki International Club at No. 7 Dejima, as well as valuable residential property in Shimonoseki, in all one of the largest private holdings of a foreign family in the country.

Japan of course was not the only one seizing the private property of enemy nationals. Until 1949, when the custom was finally banned by the Fourth Geneva Convention, countries at war were free to confiscate private property. Around the same time the Ringer family fled Japan, thousands of Japanese Americans were forced to abandon their homes and property and endure incarceration.

In early April, the Nagasaki Legal Affairs Bureau followed the directives of Imperial Ordinance No. 272 and created a real estate register—similar to those held by Japanese landowners—for each lot in the former Nagasaki Foreign Settlement subject until now to a perpetual lease. [92] Dated May 19, 1942, the first entry in the land register for No. 14 Minamiyamate shows Alcidie Ringer's daughter Alcidie Jennie Bjergfelt as the sole owner of the property. Why the elder Alcidie—who had succeeded all the interests of her husband at the time of his death in 1940 and was still in Japan when the land register was created—is not the designated landowner remains unclear. One explanation may be that, after her arrest, Alcidie had tried to avoid the seizure of the house as enemy property by transferring ownership to her daughter, who held neutral Danish nationality by right of marriage.

In a notification dated September 17, 1942, the Japanese government appointed a former Holme, Ringer & Co. clerk named Sakurama Kikuji to dispose of the movable and immovable property of the Ringer family in Nagasaki and to deposit the proceeds in a special account opened according to government orders at the Yokohama Specie Bank—albeit without the knowledge or consent of Ringer family members. While war raged in Europe and Asia, Sakurama sold or rented the lots held by the Ringer family in the former Nagasaki Foreign Settlement and found buyers for various possessions, including furniture, clothing and other personal effects as well as government bonds and even a stock of wine and gin left in the storage chamber behind the house at No. 14 Minamiyamate.

The contents of the disposed property, along with the names of buyers and amounts of money earned, can be determined from depositions submitted by Sakurama Kikuji to Allied Occupation forces after World War II and preserved today at the U. S. National Archives

---

92 The land registers are preserved today at the Nagasaki Legal Affairs Bureau as *kyūtochidaichō* (old land registers).

in Maryland.[93] The government bonds kept by Alcidie Ringer were sold to Nagasaki Shōken Shōji Gōmei Co., the wine and gin to the Nagasaki Prefecture Foreign Affairs Department, and a cache of gold coins and foreign paper currency to the Yokohama Specie Bank.

These transactions indicate that No. 14 Minamiyamate had been seized as enemy property no differently than either No. 2 Minamiyamate or the former Holme, Ringer & Co. office at No. 7 Ōura, and that Alcidie Jennie Bjergfelt, who was still in Yokohama with her husband and sons at the time, had no say in the negotiations.

Kawanami Industries

The next entry in the land register, dated March 29, 1943, shows the transfer of ownership of No. 14 Minamiyamate to three Japanese men identified as Kawanami Tahachirō, Kawahara Kinsuke and Ueno Sotojirō. Kawanami Tahachirō was director of the Imari Plant of Kawanami Industries and an older brother of company president Kawanami Toyosaku. Kawahara Kinsaku, Toyosaku's father-in-law, was the company auditor. Ueno Sotojirō was a lawyer employed in an executive position at Kawanami Industries.

Three Kawanami brothers. (Left to right) Tatsuzō, Tahachirō and Toyosaku. Tahachirō was one of the three new owners of No. 14 Minamiyamate. (from the autobiography of Kawanami Toyosaku)

---

[93] GHQ-SCAP files, NARA Record Group 331, Box 3989

A native of Toyama Prefecture, Kawanami Toyosaku had established Kawanami Industries in 1931 and succeeded in the manufacture of canned tomatoes and sardines. Later, he expanded into the glass and soda industries. In 1936, he purchased the defunct Matsuo Shipyard on Kōyagi Island near Nagasaki and pushed to the forefront of local business and industry. As an ultranationalist, Kawanami enjoyed popularity among military officers and politicians, including Japanese Imperial Army General and wartime Prime Minister Tōjō Hideki. Tōjō visited Nagasaki in March 1942 at the height of Japan's military triumphs abroad and called at the Kawanami Kōyagi Shipyard, where he praised Kawanami for his achievements in the promotion of wartime shipbuilding and urged the shipyard workers to strive for victory.[94] The relationship of the two men was so close that, during Tōjō's incarceration for war crimes after World War II, the former prime minister's wife and children took refuge in the Kawanami house in Tokyo.

Kawanami Toyosaku (1902-1968)
(Below) Kawanami Kōyagi Shipyard during World War II. (Nagasaki Institute of Applied Science)

---

[94] Nagasaki City Chronology, 186

Death in the Jungle

The circumstances of the sale of the two Ringer family houses (No. 2 and No. 14 Minamiyamate) remain as unclear as everything else surrounding the wartime status of the historic buildings. A Kawanami family descendant states that Kawanami Toyosaku did not come forward to purchase the houses but rather acquiesced to a request for cooperation from government authorities and furthermore that none of the Kawanami family members ever lived in the two houses.[95]

The land registers for No. 2 Minamiyamate and the former Holme, Ringer & Co. office at No. 7 Ōura show the transfer of ownership of the two properties to Kawanami Industries on the same day—May 7, 1943—some five weeks after the transfer of No. 14 Minamiyamate to the three Kawanami family members named above. The custodian, Sakurama Kikuji, of course conducted the transactions without consulting the Ringer family. In fact, he could not have reached them even if he had tried. Vanya Ringer had been killed in action at the Battle of River Slim in Malaysia the previous year, and his brother Michael had been taken prisoner-of-war en route to Java. Sydney and Aileen Ringer meanwhile were languishing in a civilian concentration camp in Shanghai, oblivious to either the fate of their sons or the status of their properties in Japan.

In August 1943, Kawanami Industries also acquired the rights to the telephones remaining in the former Ringer houses. Records show that three telephones changed hands for 600 yen each, the money going into the Yokohama Specie Bank accounts via Sakurama Kikuji. The new owners of No. 14 Minamiyamate (Kawanami Tahachirō, Kawahara Kinsuke and Ueno Sotojirō) assumed ownership of the two telephones in that house, while Kawanami Toyosaku took over the one at No. 2 Minamiyamate. The wording of the two Japanese documents is identical, indicating once again that No. 14 Minamiyamate and No. 2 Minamiyamate were sold as enemy property under similar circumstances. Alcidie Jennie Bjergfelt was still living without restraint in Yokohama, but for some reason the money was not remitted directly to her as the still-legal owner of the two telephones at No. 14 Minamiyamate.

---

[95] Personal communication from Kawasaki Noriko

Alcidie Jennie Bjergfelt (nee Ringer) with her two sons, John (left) and Richard, in Yokohama in 1943. Although British, Alcidie was able to remain unhindered in Japan while her husband Folmer, a neutral Dane, assisted in the transfer of Great Northern Telegraph facilities to Japan. (Private collection).

Alcidie and Folmer Bjergfelt and their two infant sons passed through Nagasaki in October 1943 on their way from Yokohama to Shanghai, the last Ringer family members to see the city. They stayed at the Golden Eagle Hotel, a Western-style hostelry near the waterfront dating back to the foreign settlement years. Despite her official exemption from enemy status, Alcidie probably had little freedom to visit familiar places, particularly the Minamiyamate hillside which overlooked the Mitsubishi Nagasaki Shipyard and other sensitive military facilities. There is no evidence to suggest that she met with Kawanami officials or even former Holme, Ringer & Co. staff. The family sailed safely to Shanghai on the NYK steamer *Shanghai-maru*, never knowing that the British-built ship would collide with a Japanese troop carrier on the return voyage and join its sister ship the *Nagasaki-maru*, which had detonated a Japanese-laid mine and sunk the previous year, on the bottom of the East China Sea.

The Golden Eagle Hotel at No. 42 Sagarimatsu, with the buildings of Minamiyamate in the background. Early twentieth-century picture postcard. (Private collection)

Turning Tide of War

Japan suffered devastating losses at the Battle of Midway in June 1942 and again during the Guadalcanal Campaign from August to February the following year. As the tide of war turned, domestic shipyards and factories scrambled desperately to meet the demand for munitions. The Kawanami Kōyagi Shipyard experienced an unprecedented surge, production of military transport vessels soaring from 32,761 tons in 1941 to 314,372 tons in 1944.[96] Behind the huge output was the sacrifice, not only of Japanese and Korean workers, but also of hundreds of Allied soldiers and sailors interned in the Fukuoka No. 2 Prisoner-of War Camp, established on Kōyagi Island within trudging distance of the shipyard. Production at the Kawanami Kōyagi Shipyard was second only to that of the Mitsubishi

---

[96] Maekawa Tadayoshi, *Kōyagijima ni okeru zōsensangyō no hensen* (Changes in the Shipbuilding Industry on Kōyagi Island) (*Keiei to Keizai*, 1969), 58

137

Nagasaki Shipyard, still plainly visible from the former Ringer and Glover residences on the Minamiyamate hillside.

The manner in which the two former Ringer houses in Minamiyamate were used during the war remains unrecorded. Just as the former Glover House at No. 3 Minamiyamate, although ostensibly owned by Mitsubishi, served as a meeting place for naval personnel, it is likely that Kawanami Toyosaku provided both No. 14 and No. 2 Minamiyamate for military purposes. Sakurama Kikuji had rented No. 4 Minamiyamate, a former Ringer property situated nearby, to the Nagasaki Fortress Headquarters (Kempeitai military police). No. 5 Minamiyamate, the site of the former Russian Consulate, had also been taken over by Nagasaki Fortress Headquarters, just as the driveway leading into No. 14 Minamiyamate had been commandeered for the exclusive use of military vehicles. The vistas once enjoyed by the Ringer family and other Europeans relaxing in their Minamiyamate gardens were now being viewed through army surveillance binoculars and the finders of three-inch guns waiting to fire on intruders.

By early 1944, American forces were pressing northward with growing ferocity, taking one Pacific island after another and inching ever closer to the Japanese archipelago. On April 11, B29 bombers attacked Nagasaki for the first time, dropping incendiary bombs into the night sky above the city. The damage was light: only thirteen people were killed and less than a dozen houses destroyed, and the Mitsubishi Nagasaki Shipyard and other industrial facilities emerged unscathed. The situation changed little over the following months. Perhaps because of its addition to the list of potential atomic bomb targets, Nagasaki remained exempt from the carpet bombings leveling other major Japanese cities. The populace just watched in terror morning and evening as B29 formations passed high over the city on their way to other targets.

The Japanese workers, Korean conscripts and Allied prisoners-of-war toiling away at the Mitsubishi factories nevertheless had to keep a watchful eye on the sky because American Hellcats conducted sting raids, flying in pairs over the eastern suburbs of the city, stalling their engines above Mt. Nabekanmuri and streaking low over Nagasaki Harbor to strafe the shipyard, scattering spent machine-gun cartridges onto the rooftops and gardens of Minami-yamate.

After the near total subjugation of Japanese forces at Iwojima and Okinawa, the Japanese government announced a reduction in rations of staples and encouraged the consumption of alternative foods such as acorns, tea dregs and dandelions. Pumpkin stalks, tree bark, potato vines and other fare considered inedible before were now a common sight on Nagasaki dinner tables.

Except for the irritation of minor air raids, the Nagasaki factories were able to continue their frantic efforts to squeeze torpedoes and *kamikaze* airplane parts from dwindling resources. With the supply of iron ore and other metals from abroad severed and domestic production crippled by the depleted workforce, Japan stripped itself of anything and everything metallic, from centuries-old temple bells to samurai swords, car bumpers and kitchen utensils. Among the first things to go in Nagasaki were the fences, plaques and other iron embellishments in the international cemeteries, a sad irony considering that some of the desecrated graves belonged to foreigners who had helped to establish Japan's modern industries.

On August 8, 1945 the citizens of Nagasaki conducted their usual monthly observance of the "Day of the Great Imperial Edict," that is, the anniversary of the December 8, 1941 declaration of war. The newspapers of this day carried front page articles informing readers that a small B29 squadron had attacked the city of Hiroshima on August 6 with a "new-type bomb" and inflicted considerable damage on the city. The frequency of air raids was such that few Nagasaki citizens took special note of the news

But the following day around 11:00 a.m., a B29 bomber nicknamed *Bockscar* released an object by parachute into the sky over Nagasaki. A few seconds later, a brilliant flash of light filled the sky and a wave of intense heat pummeled the city streets, followed by a thunderous explosion and violent blast of wind. The *Bockscar*, light now after dropping the second atomic bomb on Japan, disappeared to the south.

While the stone bungalow at No. 14 Minamiyamate, located several kilometers from the hypocenter, escaped with broken windows and tiles ripped from the roof, the entire northern section of Nagasaki was reduced to a charred wasteland, veiled from the rest of the city by a huge column of smoke, dirt and blood that reached up to the sky and sullied the clouds.

The atomic wasteland seen from the sky soon after the atomic bombing, looking south toward Nagasaki Harbor. The dark patch in the center is the ruins of Mitsubishi factories stretching along the bank of Urakami River. (Nagasaki Atomic Bomb Museum)

Chapter 6
Postwar Aftermath

Warships carrying the Second Marine Division of the U. S. Sixth Army arrived in Nagasaki Harbor on September 23, 1945 and pulled up alongside Dejima Wharf, which only a few years earlier had bustled with the arrival and departure of the Nagasaki-Shanghai steamers. At night, the entire city was shrouded in darkness because the electrical grid had still not been restored. Other essential facilities such as water and gas supply lines, hospitals, schools, transportation, banks, and government offices languished in a state of paralysis. The northern half of the city exposed directly to the atomic bombing was so devastated that it was difficult to discern even the line of former streets. The remains of Mitsubishi steelworks and arms factories marched up the Urakami valley, a silent tangle of iron frames twisted wildly out of shape. The ruins of a few reinforced concrete buildings crouched in the wasteland as though battered with a gigantic hammer. Survivors were still sleeping in cave shelters and searching for the remains of loved ones. Tallies taken at the end of the year would show that more than 150,000 people, or two-thirds of the population of Nagasaki, had been killed or injured as a result of the explosion of a single atomic bomb. The stench of death hung in the air as though permanently imprinted there.

Above the waterfront on the Minamiyamate hillside, the former Glover House at No. 3 Minamiyamate and the former Ringer family houses at No. 2 and No. 14 Minamiyamate stood empty and deserted. The house at No. 9 Minamiyamate occupied by Kuraba Tomisaburō and his wife since the sale of the Glover House was also steeped in silence. Waka had died during the war, and Tomisaburō had committed suicide on August 26, less than a month before the arrival of American forces, bringing a tragic end to the Glover family presence in Nagasaki dating back to the opening of the port in 1859.

The house at No. 14 Minamiyamate escaped the brunt of the atomic bomb explosion, but its windows were broken and roof tiles ripped off. (Courtesy of Nagasaki City)

The first item on the Allied agenda was the release of prisoners-of-war stranded in former POW camps in the Nagasaki area, including Fukuoka No. 2 Camp on Kōyagi Island where some 500 British, American, Australian and Dutch prisoners, finally freed from forced labor at the Kawanami Kōyagi Shipyard, waited for repatriation. The next priority was the disarmament of the country and the destruction of all weapons and other instruments of war. Most of the Mitsubishi arms factories lay demolished in the aftermath of the atomic bombing, and production at both the Mitsubishi Nagasaki Shipyard and Kawanami Kōyagi Shipyard had ground to a halt after Japan's defeat in the war.

The Sixth Army requisitioned a large number of buildings to billet officers and soldiers coming ashore. The Western-style buildings in the former foreign settlement of course provided ideal accommodations and were promptly earmarked for requisition, any Japanese people occupying them given short order to evacuate. Before the end of the month, the Americans had added the former Glover residence at No. 3 Minamiyamate and the former Ringer family house at No. 14 Minamiyamate to the list of appropriated buildings. By now, the Japanese army personnel who had been using the buildings during the war were long gone.

Among the American officers spearheading the occupation of Nagasaki was Captain Joseph C. Goldsby, a native of Florida who had graduated in civil engineering from the University of Florida and continued his studies at Harvard, the University of Virginia and the University of California. Goldsby arrived in Nagasaki as an engineer with the 5th Amphibious Corps Military Government Staff and played an important role in restoring infrastructure and essential services in the war-ravaged city. His leading position among his fellow officers is indicated by the fact that he was able to choose one of the most desirous buildings in Nagasaki as a private residence: the historic colonial-style stone bungalow at No. 14 Minamiyamate.[97]

Barbara Goldsby and Madame Butterfly House

Goldsby's wife Barbara joined her husband in Nagasaki a year after the initial occupation. The Second Marine Division had completed its mission of disarming Japan and was now being replaced by a body called the Nagasaki Military Government Team (NMGT) established to help local government restore industrial, cultural and educational facilities. A fellow native of Florida, she joined her husband at No. 14 Minamiyamate, riding imported military vehicles up the winding road from the base of the hillside and parking them in the bay on the north side of the house once reserved for the Ringer family's Packard.

Joseph and Barbara Goldsby engaged Japanese maids and gardeners to cater to their daily needs and to maintain the house and garden. The presence of Occupation personnel on the hillside, while bringing relief from the tyranny of Japanese military police, may have reminded some elderly residents of the years in the nineteenth century when foreigners, bolstered by huge economic advantages, cut themselves off from the local community and stubbornly upheld their European way of life on the elevated terraces.

---

[97] Lane R. Earns, "Victor's Justice: Colonel Victor Delnore and the U. S. Occupation of Nagasaki," *Crossroads: A Journal of Nagasaki History and Culture,* No. 3, Summer 1995, 83

American Occupation personnel with Japanese children in Nagasaki. Joseph Goldsby is standing on the right behind his wife Barbara (white dress). The couple were the last foreign residents of both the former Glover House and the stone bungalow at No. 14 Minamiyamate. (Private collection)

Goldsby served later as chief of the Economics Section in the NMGT. He was discharged from the Army on August 12, 1947 with the rank of colonel but remained in Nagasaki as an army civilian. NMGT personnel lists and telephone registers show Joseph and Barbara Goldsby still living at No. 14 Minamiyamate in July 1947 but moving the following year to the former Glover House at No. 3 Minamiyamate, where they famously invented and perpetuated the fallacious nickname "Madame Butterfly House."[98] Later transferred to Osaka, Joseph C. Goldsby is listed as a member of the Osaka Reserve Officer Association in the March 28, 1950 issue of the U. S. military newspaper *Pacific Stars and Stripes*.

---

[98] For further information see: Brian Burke-Gaffney, *The Glover House of Nagasaki: An Illustrated History* (Flying Crane Press, 2016)

One of the Japanese citizens monitoring the American presence in Nagasaki was Kawanami Toyosaku. At the time of the atomic bombing and Japan's surrender, the energetic industrialist had been staying in his family house in the Nishiyama neighborhood of Nagasaki. Now he was contending with the collapse of Kawanami Industries and accusations from Allied investigators that he had been responsible for the death and mistreatment of the POWs forced to toil in his shipyard. Although excused of war crimes, Kawanami was added to a list of thousands of war sympathizers banished from positions of leadership in government and industry in the wake of a purge conducted by the General Headquarters of the Supreme Command of the Allied Powers (GHQ-SCAP).

Heartbreak and Disgust

In March 1946, GHQ-SCAP established a unit called the Civil Property Custodian (CPC) to conduct an investigation regarding the assets owned by Allied civilians but frozen or sold off by the Japanese government during the war. In July 1947, Cooper Blyth, representative of the UK Reparations and Restitution Mission, wrote to the CPC with regard to the Ringer family properties, which constituted one of the largest private holdings under review. The letter is preserved today along with hundreds of related documents at the U. S. National Archives and Records Administration (NARA) in College Park, Maryland, the huge volume of files indicating the complicated mass of problems associated with the identification, assessment and retrieval of the Ringer properties.[99]

Soon after posting the letter, Blyth pressed the custodian Sakurama Kikuji for information and engaged Japanese auditors to compile a list of the possessions removed from the houses at No. 2 and No. 14 Minamiyamate. Dated August 25, 1947 and entitled "Articles and Fixtures at No. 14 Minamiyamate-machi, Nagasaki," the three-page list submitted by the auditors regarding the latter property describes most of the items "owned by Mrs. Alcidie Eva Ringer when they were taken by the Japanese government"— including silverware and dinner cutlery for eighty people, a dressing table with tortoiseshell brushes, and eighty-five framed paintings—

---

[99] "Ringer Property Vol. I and II" (NARA, RG331, Box 3989)

as "whereabouts unknown after A-bomb explosion." Except for one intricately carved table with curved legs kept by a granddaughter of Kawahara Kinsuke (Kawanami Toyosaku's father-in-law), the destination of Alcidie Ringer's personal effects remains unknown to this day.

With regard to real estate, Sakurama Kikuji provided a list of sixteen lots in the former Nagasaki Foreign Settlement including the house at No. 2 Minamiyamate, the former Holme, Ringer & Co. office at No. 7 Ōura, and the former Nagasaki International Club at No. 7 Dejima. Oddly enough, he did not add No. 14 Minamiyamate to the list. When asked about the omission, Sakurama insisted that the house had been sold before the war. The statement was patently false, but for some reason the issue of the house and land at No. 14 Minamiyamate did not provoke any further discussion. Cooper Blyth employed a Japanese photographer to visit the Ringer properties and record their current state. The resulting collection of annotated monochrome photographs provides an invaluable record of the buildings owned by the Ringer family in Nagasaki and Shimonoseki. But the collection does not include a single shot of Alcidie's former residence at No. 14 Minamiyamate.

Sometime in the early postwar period, whether out of heartbreak and disgust over the loss of her prized property or out of sheer fatigue, the now seventy-year-old Alcidie Eva Ringer apparently decided to collect only the proceeds from bank accounts and the sale of property and to relinquish any claim to the house and land at No. 14 Minamiyamate. In a legal document signed in a lawyer's office in London on December 15, 1950, she gave her brother-in-law Sydney Ringer power of attorney to dispose of her interests in Japan. Sydney submitted a demand to GHQ-SCAP for compensation regarding Alcidie's personal belongings, delineated under four headings as "cash and deposits," "shares and bonds," "household effects and personal property" and "other assets."

A Japanese lawyer in Osaka drew up a final report in June 1951, including a table of all the income and expenditures involved in the disposal of the property. The table shows a total income of 32,743.35 yen and total expenditures of 31,287.03 yen. The latter includes a sum of 27,840 yen withdrawn by Sydney on March 20, 1951, undoubtedly for remittance to Alcidie Ringer in England. The case of No. 14 Minamiyamate rested there.

Alcidie Eva Ringer (far right) poses for a photograph with her daughter Alcidie and grandson in England after World War II. The man on the left is her son-in-law Folmer Bjergfelt. The name of the woman second from left is unknown. Alcidie Eva Ringer died in London in 1955 without ever returning to Japan. (Private collection)

Mountain Lodge Club

Another gap opens in the history of the grand stone bangalow at No. 14 Minamiyamate after the departure of American Occupation personnel circa 1948. Kawanami Kōyagi Shipyard resumed operation in March the same year, serving as a facility for the manufacture and repair of fishing boats and other small vessels, but little is known about how and when the house at No. 14 Minamiyamate was returned to Kawanami Industries.

A rough map of the neighborhood drawn up in May 1949 identifies the house at No. 14 Minamiyamate as the "Sansō Kurabu" (Mountain Lodge Club).[100] No other information is available to shed light on this rather odd appellation, but the use of the word *kurabu*, rendered with Chinese characters, indicates that Kawanami Industries provided—or planned to provide—the building as a place of rest and recreation for company employees after the relaunching of the company. Interestingly, the map shows three other buildings on the site, identified as the houses of Ueno Sotojirō (co-owner of No. 14 Minamiyamate), Kawahara Murashige (brother-in-law of Kawanami Toyosaku), and Saikawa Yoshio (relationship unknown), presumably erected soon after the Americans left.

The career of No. 14 Minamiyamate as a clubhouse probably did not last for very long. Beset with labor disputes and deep in debt, Kawanami Industries declared bankruptcy in 1950, laid off all of its 4,792 workers, and initiated liquidation proceedings in the Nagasaki District Court that would drag on for several years.[101]

Although no exact record exists, Kawanami employees or other people with connections to the company apparently occupied the Minamiyamate house, quickly transforming it into a grungy tenement. A Japanese book on Meiji-period architecture published in 1965 mentions that the building at No. 14 Minamiyamate, referred to as the "Ringer Older Brother House," was in use at the time as a Kawanami dormitory.[102]

The Western-style buildings in the former Nagasaki Foreign Settlement would soon be recognized for their unique architectural features and exotic flavor, but during the first years after the end of World War II, they were little more than convenient receptacles for the bedraggled multitudes struggling to survive in the atomic-bombed, economically stagnant city.

---

[100] *Nagasaki-shi sansō kurabu fukin jissoku heimenzu* (Survey Plan of the Mountain Lodge Club and vicinity, Nagasaki City), preserved at Glover Garden, Nagasaki

[101] Kamura Kunio et al, ed., *Nagasaki jiten sangyō shakai hen* (Nagasaki Dictionary: Industry and Society), (Nagasaki Bunkensha, 1989), 150-1. The shipyard later resumed operation but soon closed permanently.

[102] Sakamoto Katsuhiko, *Meiji no ijinkan* (Foreign Residences of the Meiji Period) (Asahi Shimbunsha, 1965), 13

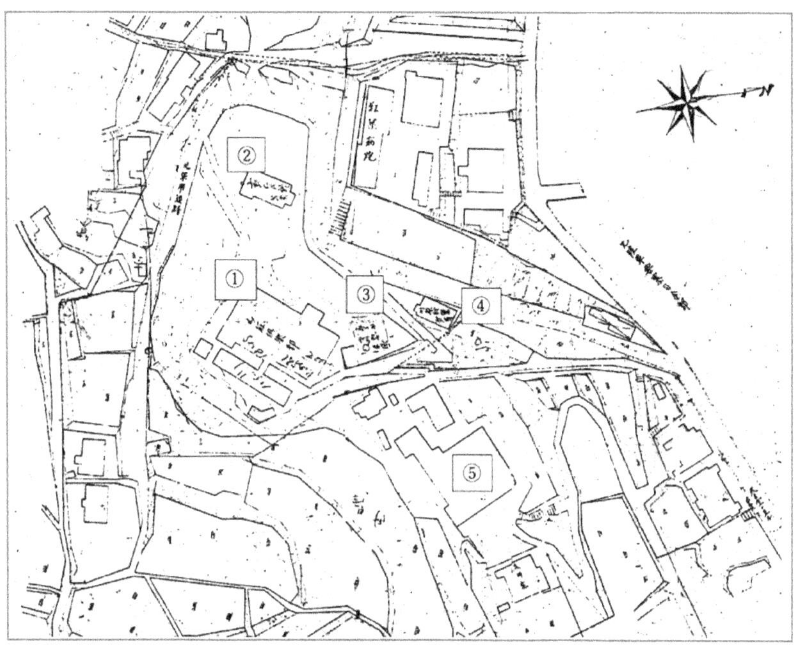

Map of Minamiyamate dated May 1949, when the former Ringer family houses at No. 14 and No. 2 were under Kawanami ownership. 1) Sansō Kurabu (Mountain Lodge Club) at No. 14 Minamiyamate, 2) house of Ueno Sotojirō, 3) house of Saikawa Yoshio, 4) house of Kawahara Murashige, 5) former Ringer House at No. 2 Minamiyamate. (Glover Garden)

Five Families in my Pantry

When Sydney and Aileen Ringer finally returned to Nagasaki in February 1951, they found a city dramatically changed during the decade of their absence. The former foreign settlement had not suffered any severe damage because of its distance from the atomic bomb hypocenter and the protection of hills and canals, but many of the old Western-style buildings had been deliberately demolished during the war to create fire breaks, including buildings on rear lots owned by the Ringer family. One dear to the hearts of Sydney and Aileen, the Holme, Ringer & Co. office at No. 7 Ōura, had fallen victim to fire, although the conflagration had occurred, not while Kawanami

Industries used it as an office during the war, but in April 1947 when the Occupation forces set up an officers' club there. All that remained in 1951 was a weed-infested empty lot strewn with scorched roof-tile fragments and bricks from the broken chimneys.

The former Ringer residence at No. 2 Minamiyamate, meanwhile, was in a state of chaos. More than three years had passed since GHQ-SCAP ordered investigations concerning the Ringer properties, but the process of restitution was still mired in a tangle of red tape, one of the most prickly issues being the eviction of squatters.

The Ringer House at No. 2 Minamiyamate in a photograph taken by American Occupation personnel in July 1947. The house still shows signs of damage from the atomic-bomb blast. The presence of squatters is indicated by the washing hanging out to dry and the front lawn plowed to cultivate vegetables. Sydney and Aileen Ringer would find the house in a similar derelict state when they returned to Nagasaki in 1951. (U. S. National Archives)

On April 27, Sydney sent a message to the UK Reparations and Restitution Mission in Tokyo, appealing as follows for assistance in restoring his rightful ownership to his house:

152

It Is my intention to live on the property known as No. 2 Minamiyamate my former private residence but can hardly do so with five families living in my pantry. This is no exaggeration. There are also one family in my kitchen and three more families in the servants' quarters and the children have already damaged the paintwork and broken the typhoon shutters.

After months of appeals and negotiations, Sydney Ringer finally succeeded in regaining possession of the family properties in Nagasaki and Shimonoseki. The rights to the house at No. 2 Minamiyamate were transferred back to Sydney from Kawanami Industries in May 1954, and repairs were conducted at the expense of the Japanese government. The stone bungalow at No. 14 Minamiyamate meanwhile remained in the hands of the Kawanami family, uncontested by its original bonafide owners Alcidie Eva Ringer and her daughter, ignored by British and American authorities, and gradually sinking into a state of disrepair.

Sydney apparently planned to live in Japan, but his hopes were dashed the following year when his wife Eileen committed suicide at her son's house in Yorkshire. Alcidie Eva Ringer died in London the same year, without ever returning to Nagasaki or seeing her former home. Sydney later arranged for the disposal of all the family properties in Japan. No. 7 Ōura, where the Holme, Ringer & Co. office had stood, was sold to the Nagasaki Jidōsha Co. in 1952. Nagasaki City purchased the former Nagasaki International Club at No. 7 Dejima for a municipal museum and the land in the rear quarter of Ōura for use as a junior high school. No. 4 Minamiyamate went to the Regional Government Employees Union and was converted into a recreation facility. No. 10B Minamiyamate, site of the former Nagasaki Bowling Club, was later cleared of buildings and made into a car park.

The last property to go was the house at No. 2 Minamiyamate, sold to Nagasaki City in 1965 for eighteen million yen.[103] Designated a National Important Cultural Property the following year, the building was opened to the public along with the former Glover House, which had been donated to Nagasaki City in 1957 by Mitsubishi Heavy Industries. Sydney Ringer died in England in 1967.

---

[103] Nagasaki City Chronology, 291

Thirteen Stakeholders

The land register shows a further change in the ownership of No. 14 Minamiyamate on October 14, 1955. The one-third owned by Kawahara Kinsaku was divided into six portions to be held by his wife and five children, including his daughter Harue, wife of Kawanami Toyosaku. Five days later, the one-third owned by Kawanami Tahachirō (Toyosaku's older brother) was similarly divided, the largest portion going to his daughter Chio and five smaller portions going to his three sons and two nieces. The one-third owned by Ueno Sotojirō remained intact, bringing to thirteen the number of stakeholders in the historic building.

Washing hangs out to dry in front of the stone bungalow at No. 14 Minamiyamate during its postwar career as a tenement building. The Italianate fountain strikes an odd contrast in the foreground. (Harold S. Williams Collection, National Library of Australia)

Except for Kawahara Murashige and Ueno Sotojirō, who owned the small wooden buildings erected on the lot, none of the Kawanami family members lived in the stone bungalow at No. 14 Minamiyamate. Kawahara Kinsaku's granddaughter remembers hearing that the building was in a dilapidated state but has only vague memories of visits there.

In 1961, the family suffered a widely publicized setback when police arrested Kawanami Toyosaku for involvement in a botched *coup d'état* and assassination attempt, a disturbance remembered today as the Sanmu Incident. Kawanami served a two-year prison sentence and then retreated to his house in Tokyo, where he died on December 11, 1968. Kawanami Industries, meanwhile, sputtered along until finally putting the Kōyagi shipyard up for public sale in 1965. No takers appeared, but Mitsubishi Heavy Industries finally purchased the woebegone shipyard the following year and added it to its rapidly growing industrial facilities.

Forgotten and Neglected

The ragtag assembly of people still inhabiting the house at No. 14 Minamiyamate adapted the building to their needs, covering the hardwood floors with tatami mats, plugging the fireplaces to keep out draughts, and enclosing the veranda in windowed panels. Some of them attached additions, slipshod wooden structures that looked like tumors growing on the old walls. While preserving some privacy by turning the parlors and bedrooms into separate apartments, they shared toilets, baths and kitchen facilities and took turns cleaning and sweeping. Children played happily in the front garden and commuted to the nearby elementary school. Aside from the unusual features of the building, little remained of the years when foreigners inhabited the house.

Nagasaki photographer Kobayashi Masaru visited the house at No. 14 Minamiyamate in April 1966 and took snapshots of the front and rear of the building, capturing invaluable glimpses of the property as it languished—forgotten by former foreign residents and neglected by its new owners—between the gloom of war and the development of Minamiyamate as a tourist attraction. In his caption to the photographs, Kobayashi reports simply that: "Several families had been living in the house since after the war."[104]

---

[104] Kobayashi Masaru, *Nagasaki no meiji yōkan* (Nagasaki Western-style Buildings of the Meiji Period) (Nagasaki, 1993), 197

Photographs of the stone bungalow at No. 14 Minamiyamate taken by Kobayashi Masaru in 1966. The house was still a makeshift apartment building occupied by Japanese families. (Above) The veranda has been enclosed with glass panels to provide living space. (Below) The kitchen and servants' quarters at the rear of the main house have also been converted for everyday use.

156

Chapter 7
Yesterday and Today

I n 1957, Mitsubishi Nagasaki Shipyard donated the former Glover House and the surrounding 4,800 square-meter plot of land to Nagasaki City to commemorate the 100th anniversary of its predecessor, the Nagasaki Iron Foundry, established with the help of Dutch engineers in 1857. The following year, the former Glover House was opened to the public and quickly attracted attention in Japan and abroad as a symbol of Nagasaki's history of international exchange and its unique eclectic culture.

Despite the name, however, the building was better known as "Madame Butterfly House" than as the former residence of British entrepreneur Thomas B. Glover. Reporting on the opening of the house, the newspaper *Illustrated London News* published a photograph of a young Japanese woman in the garden with the headline "Japan—On a hill facing the harbour in Nagasaki: Madame Butterfly's House, which now belongs to the local government authority."[105] The frivolous *Madame Butterfly House* nickname coined by American Occupation personnel had become an established catch-phrase in Nagasaki's postwar tourism industry.

In June 1961, the Japanese government designated the former Glover House a National Important Cultural Property, primarily for its architectural value as the oldest Western-style building in Japan. As long as Nagasaki City carefully preserved the physical structure, the Japanese Agency for Cultural Affairs did not object to the use of the Madame Butterfly theme in the promotion of tourism. Systematic historical/cultural research had still not begun in 1966 when the former residence of Sydney Ringer and family at No.

---

[105] *The Illustrated London News*, August 23, 1958

159

2 Minamiyamate was also recognized for its architectural value and designated a National Important Cultural Property.

The two houses were open for a fee to the public, but the patchwork of other stately Western-style buildings and gardens on the hillside remained mostly unchanged, hiding in the shade of old camphor and gingko trees like the cast-off shells of long-departed insects. One friend of the Ringer family, who revisited Minamiyamate in the 1960s, described the setting as follows:

> For an hour or two I wandered around the haunts of the old foreign community in Nagasaki—above and below Minami-yamate—and my sensitivity to atmosphere responded readily. Largely unaffected by the hand of time, there were all the old monuments. Huge retaining walls, steep ramps, glimpses of dignified residences cloaked with trees and unmodernized, quiet and relatively trafficless roads, peopled by unidentifiable ghosts.[106]

But the situation was changing rapidly. A swelling torrent of Japanese tourists, foreign travelers and children on school excursions was flocking to the former Glover House and Ringer House, attracted by the references to Madame Butterfly and other romantic if whimsical themes. The money they dropped along the way filled the pockets of government bodies, hotel owners and souvenir vendors and helped fuel the recovery of Nagasaki from the devastation of World War II. Tourism now ranked with shipbuilding and fisheries as a vital Nagasaki industry.

Inspired by the huge success of Meiji Village—an outdoor architectural museum opened in 1965 in Aichi Prefecture to relocate and preserve nineteenth-century buildings from around Japan—Nagasaki City announced plans to fence off a large swath of Minamiyamate hillside centering around the former Glover House and former Ringer House and to emulate Meiji Village by relocating other Western-style buildings to the open spaces nearby. The imitation was such that, during the planning stages, the theme park garnered the temporary name "Nagasaki Meiji Village."

---

[106] Arnold Graham to Harold S. Williams, 16 December 1968 (H.S. Williams Collection, National Library of Australia, MS 6681/2/33)

160

An aerial photograph taken in September 1962 by the Geospacial Information Authority of Japan (MKU-62-8-C11B-2) captures the Minamiyamate hillside. (1) No. 14 Minamiyamate, still inhabited by former Kawanami employees. The small Japanese houses erected in the garden are visible, including (2) the house of Ueno Sotojirō; (3) the house of Sydney Ringer; (4) the former Glover house, designated a National Important Cultural Property the previous year.

The Former Alt House

Nagasaki City naturally turned its attention to the "Ringer Older Brother House" at No. 14 Minamiyamate, standing adjacent to the former Ringer House, still privately owned and inhabited by a large number of tenants. City officials contacted Kawanami Toyosaku, explained the plans for a Nagasaki version of Meiji Village, and requested his cooperation. However, Kawanami refused to sell the property, insisting that, "Since I demolished my house in Nishiyama, I want to make [No. 14 Minamiyamate] my Nagasaki residence in the future." The anecdote is interesting because it suggests that, even though he was not one of the official owners, the former president of Kawanami Industries looked at No. 14 Minamiyamate as his personal property and dreamed of living there someday.

After Kawanami's death in December 1968, Nagasaki City contacted the bereaved family and reiterated the request for cooperation. Kawahara Isao, the eldest son of Kawahara Kinsaku and brother-in-law of Kawanami Toyosaku, stepped forward to represent the family. In a handwritten memorandum dated April 17, 1969, Kawahara agreed on behalf of the owners to begin negotiations with the city. Entitled *Minamiyamate-machi jūyonbankan kankei shorui* (Documents Regarding No. 14 Minamiyamate), the related documents give the names and addresses of owners and provide information on the buildings erected later on the lot. They also outline the complex status of the property, including the fact that a large number of people were still living in the historic building and that the road leading up the hillside had been provided for public automobile traffic.[107]

Nagasaki city officials met with the owners and worked out an agreement regarding terms of sale. Arrangements were also made to compensate the families faced with eviction and to purchase and demolish the smaller buildings erected on the lot. In an official contract signed on March 31, 1970, the owners of No. 14 Minami-yamate, represented by Kawahara Isao, agreed to sell the property comprising buildings and land (6,131.87 square meters or about 1,855 *tsubo* in area) to Nagasaki City for a total of 74,195,627 yen—more than four times the amount paid to Sydney Ringer for No. 2 Minamiyamate.

Workers immediately removed all the refuse, decorations and unwanted structures accumulated over the years. Investigations regarding the architectural features of the house ensued, and in May 1972 the Japanese Agency for Cultural Affairs designated the building a National Important Cultural Property, a recognition second only to National Treasure. The official name applied to the property was "Former Alt House" based on evidence identifying William J. Alt as the builder and original inhabitant. The reason for the designation is cited as follows on the Agency for Cultural Affairs website:

> The house is a single-story building of stone construction with Tuscan-style stone pillars arranged along a veranda as well as a portico with a gabled roof protruding at the front. It is among

---

[107] Preserved today at Glover Garden along with other official documents.

the oldest and most elaborately designed Western-style houses in Nagasaki. It is also unusual in that an early floor plan categorizes the use of each room at the time of construction. The annex and storeroom of brick construction situated at the rear of the main building, which date to the middle of the Meiji Period, provide an invaluable, well-preserved example of the subsidiary structures of early Western-style houses in Nagasaki.[108]

The Birth of Glover Garden

The Minamiyamate theme park took shape in two phases from early 1970, soon after the sale of the former Alt House to Nagasaki City. Workers constructed outdoor ponds, murals and walkways, built gardens, and installed an unusual outdoor escalator to carry visitors up the hillside. A large modern hotel opened nearby to answer the demand for upscale accommodations, and a gauntlet of souvenir shops sprouted along the old flagstone approach. Nagasaki City held a naming contest and selected "Glover Garden" from among 190 suggestions submitted by citizens. Inaugurated on September 3, 1974, Glover Garden consisted of the three National Important Cultural Properties and six other historic Western-style buildings relocated from around the city.

One of the relocated buildings was the former Steele Academy, a two-story wooden school building built at No. 9 Higashiyamate in 1887 by the Dutch Reformed Church in America and donated by its current owner, Kaisei High School. For lack of another appropriate spot, the planners decided to reassemble the building in the southern corner of the former Alt House garden, near the entrance to the property from the road outside. The construction marred the National Important Cultural Property by introducing, in close proximity, a building with little historical, cultural or even architectural similarity and confusing the border between original and relocated buildings. Glover Garden gained fame throughout Japan as a symbol of Nagasaki's unique *ikokujōcho* (exotic atmos-

---

[108] https://kunishitei.bunka.go.jp/bsys/maindetails.asp (translated from Japanese by the author)

phere), welcoming thousands of visitors and bringing tourism shoulder to shoulder with shipbuilding and fisheries as a pillar of the city's postwar economy, but the question of historical authenticity remained on the back burner.

With regard to the former Alt House, the unusual style of the building remained the principal focus of attention, while pamphlets and signs devoted only a few words to the life and times of William J. Alt as the person who built the house. Memories of Henry J. Hunt and family, the years of service as the U. S. Consulate, the grand international parties held by the Ringer family during World War I, and the sad story of Alcidie Ringer's arrest and internment were mostly forgotten.

The former Alt House at No. 14 Minamiyamate was dismantled as part of the restoration project. Only the three interior chimneys remained standing.

Nagasaki City conferred with the Japanese government soon after the opening of Glover Garden and laid out plans for the restoration of the former Alt House. Experts from a subsidiary body called the Japanese Association for Conservation of Architectural Monuments (JACAM) set up an office on the site and surveyed the buildings and gardens. Starting from April 1977, workers took apart

164

the house, replaced plaster, rotten beams and broken stones, and put everything back together on the basis of blueprints from the preliminary investigation. The buildings at the rear of the main house also underwent a thoroughgoing facelift. The restoration project reached completion two years later at a total cost of 180 million yen.

The work returned the building to a pristine state but erased all the stains, odors and nuances accumulated during its turbulent 110-year history. Since nothing remained from the day in December 1941 when Japanese police knocked on the door and arrested Alcidie Eva Ringer, the planners had to augment the empty rooms with a motley assortment of old furniture and bric-a-brac brought in from elsewhere. Moreover, the rules regarding National Important Cultural Properties prohibited any alteration to the physical status of the building. Nails and tacks were out of the question, so the walls—once scattered with paintings and photographs—remained strangely blank. The long report published at the completion of the project in 1979 provides a wealth of information about the architectural features of the house, including numerous photographs that capture the state of the building before and after the restoration work, but it runs dry on the cultural history of the building.[109]

A three-page article at the end of the report is entitled "Alt's Stay in Nagasaki" but in fact dwells mostly on Ōura Kei, the Nagasaki entrepreneur who associated with foreign merchants in the export of Japanese tea in the 1860s and 1870s. It invites misunderstanding about William J. Alt by quoting from a statement made by Ōura on her deathbed, asserting, obviously incorrectly, that Alt came to Nagasaki in 1856 at the age of sixteen and "submitted a huge order" for tea leaves. This absurdity has come down unchallenged to the present day, trotted out again and again in discussions on the beginnings of the tea trade. The article also misleads readers by suggesting that Alt was involved in the Tōyama Incident. As outlined in the present work, the conflict with Kumamoto merchant Tōyama Ichiya occurred after Alt's departure from Nagasaki, during Henry J. Hunt's stint as Alt & Co. leader. In short, the article does little except to expose the lack of research on the life and work of William J. Alt and other former residents of the Nagasaki Foreign Settlement.

---

[109] Nagasaki City ed., *Kyū oruto jūtaku shūrikōji hōkokusho* (Report on the Restoration of the Former Alt House), March 1979

The entrance hall of the former Alt House in the 1930s (left) and after the completion of the restoration project in 1979. The project eradicated all remnants of the Ringer family sojourn.

An early tourist pamphlet published by Nagasaki City.

Descendants Visit the House

The remarkable profile of Alt family descendants came suddenly to light in October 1985 when Tessa and David Montgomery visited Nagasaki and met with local officials. Tessa is the granddaughter of William J. Alt's daughter Nancy, born in 1872 after the family returned to England. Her father, William J. Alt's grandson, is Lieutenant-General Frederick Browning, a World War II hero whose exploits were depicted in the 1977 epic film *A Bridge Too Far*. Tessa's mother is the noted British writer Daphne Du Maurier, author of novels such as *Rebecca* and *The Birds* made famous as Hollywood movies by Alfred Hitchcock. David Montgomery meanwhile is the son of Lieutenant-General Bernard Montgomery, who led British forces to victory at the Second Battle of El Alamein in 1942 and won admiration in postwar Britain as a war hero and member of the House of Lords granted the title Viscount Montgomery of Alamein. During her visit to Nagasaki, Tessa donated a family tree and excerpts from the memoirs of her great-grandmother, Elisabeth Alt, documents that shed a valuable new light on the family experience in Japan.

Tessa and David Montgomery, 2nd Viscount Montgomery of Alamein, in front of the former Alt House in 1985. (Courtesy of Nagasaki Newspaper Co.)

In 1991, the Japanese government designated the Minami-yamate and Higashiyamate neighborhoods historic preservation zones, ensuring the physical protection of buildings in the residential districts of the former Nagasaki Foreign Settlement. The number of visitors to Glover Garden reached a peak of over two million per year around the same time but steadily declined, due in part to an overall regression in the Nagasaki economy but also to the failure of local authorities to go beyond the description of architectural features and discuss the former Glover House, former Ringer House and former Alt House in their historical/cultural context.

The next visit of a descendant of former Alt House inhabitants came in 2010, when Richard Bjergfelt, son of Alcidie Jennie Bjergfelt (nee Ringer), was welcomed to Nagasaki with his wife Maureen during a trip to Japan. Richard had contacted Nagasaki City the previous year, offering to donate family heirlooms including silver cups won by Frederick Ringer in foot and boat races, an album of Nagasaki photographs taken by pioneer photographer Ueno Hikoma, and works of art done by his mother including the Japanese-style painting introduced in the present work (p. 119). The middle room at the rear of the house (the courtroom of the former U. S. Consulate) was allocated for the display of the artifacts, bringing a much-needed touch of connectivity to the old building.

Richard also provided a wealth of family photographs that reveal the state of the house, both inside and outside, when Freddie and Alcidie Ringer lived there a century ago. The photographs, introduced here in part, make an important contribution to research on the Nagasaki Foreign Settlement in that they provide vivid glimpses into the interior of the former Alt House. Until then, the vast majority of photographs available from the foreign settlement period depicted buildings exclusively from the outside.

Another visit went unnoticed by local government and media. Ranald Noel-Paton, great-grandson of William J. Alt, called at Nagasaki with his wife Patricia during an ocean cruise in May 2015 and paid a visit to the former Alt House in Glover Garden. Ranald's grandmother Ethyl was born in Nagasaki in 1866 at the height of William J. Alt's business activities in the waning years of the Edo Period. Ranald is the author of *An Eastern Calling: George Windsor Earl and a Vision of Empire* (Ashgrove Publishing, 2018), the biography of Alt's father-in-law cited in the present work.

Thoughts of Faraway Homelands

The former Alt House continues its vigil on the Minamiyamate hillside, watching ships crisscross Nagasaki Harbor and cantilever cranes swing slowly over the building berths at Mitsubishi Nagasaki Shipyard. Every year, more than a million visitors pay the entrance fee to Glover Garden and follow the paths to the house, where they marvel at the uncanny style of the building and peer into the cold, deserted rooms. The area around the Italianate fountain at the front often accommodates outdoor wedding ceremonies and parties catered by a local hotel, but few of the guests remember a time when British and American residents lounged on the veranda gazing at the harbor, their optimistic view of Japan complicated by a sense of cultural difference and wistful thoughts of faraway homelands.

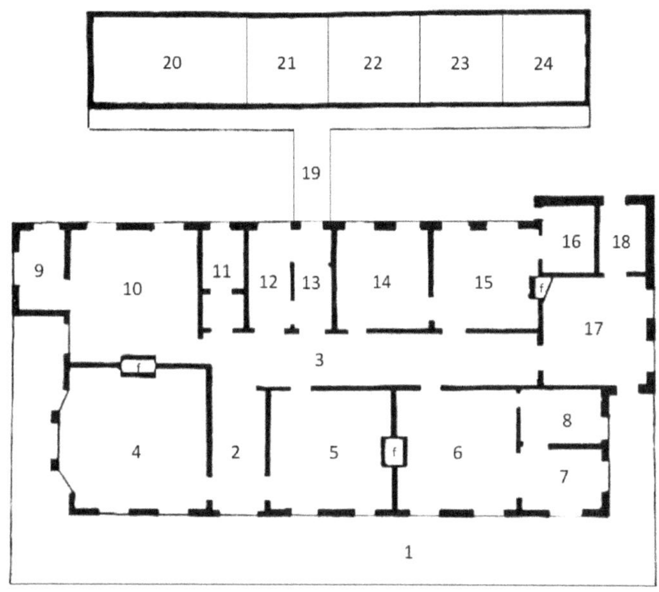

1. Veranda
2. Vestibule
3. Interior corridor
4. Living room (reception*)
5. Parlor (consul's office)
6. Master bedroom
7. Dressing room
8. Bath
9. Storage
10. Dining room (interpreter's room)
11. Lavatory
12. Storage
    f. Chimney with fireplaces

13. Corridor to the outside
14. Study (courtroom)
15. Bedroom (marshal's room)
16. Bath
17. Bedroom (unused)
18. Bath
19. Elevated outside corridor
20. Kitchen
21. Pantry
22. Servant's quarters
23. Servant's quarters
24. Storage

*   Words in parentheses show the use of the room during the U. S. Consulate period

BIBLIOGRAPHY

Alcock, Sir Rutherford. *The Capital of the Tycoon: A Narrative of a Three Years' Residence in Japan*. London: Longman, Green, Longman, Roberts, and Green, 1863.

Beasley, William G. *Great Britain and the Opening of Japan 1834-1858*. London: The Japan Library, 1995.

Burke-Gaffney, Brian. *Nagasaki: The British Experience, 1854-1945*. Folkestone: Global Oriental, 2009.
----------. *Holme, Ringer & Company: The Rise and Fall of a British Enterprise in Japan, 1868-1940*. Brill, 2013.

Chang, Richard T. *The Justice of the Western Consular Courts in Nineteenth-Century Japan*. Westport: Greenwood Press, 1984.

Cortazzi, Hugh. *Victorians in Japan in and around the Treaty Ports*. London and Atlantic Highlands, NJ: The Athlone Press, 1988.

Earns, Lane R. *Nagasaki kyoryūchi no seiyōjin* (Westerners in the Nagasaki Foreign Settlement). Nagasaki: Nagasaki Bunkensha, 2002.
----------. "The Foreign Settlement in Nagasaki, 1859-1869." *The Historian* Vol.56, No.3. Spring 1994.

Hellyer, David T. *At the Forest's Edge: Memoir of a Physician-Naturalist*. Seattle: University of Washington Press, 1985).

Iwasaki Yatarō and Iwasaki Yanosuke Biography Editorial Committee ed., *Iwasaki yatarō den* (Biography of Iwasaki Yatarō). Tokyo, 1967.

Kobayashi, Masaru. *Nagasaki meiji yōkan* (Western-style Buildings of the Meiji Period in Nagasaki). Private publication, 1993.

Kitano Norio, *Amakusa kaigai hattenshi* (History of Amakusa in Overseas Development). Fukuoka: Ashi Shobō, 1985.

McKay, Alexander. *Scottish Samurai: Thomas Blake Glover 1838-1911*. Edinburgh: Canongate Press, 1997.

Nagasaki City, ed. *Nagasaki shisei rokujūgonenshi* (A Sixty-Five-Year History of the Nagasaki Municipal Administration). Nagasaki, 1959.
----------. *Nagasaki shishi nenpyō* (Nagasaki City Chronology). Nagasaki, 1981.

----------. *Nagasaki genbaku sensaishi* (Record of the War Damages Caused by the Nagasaki Atomic Bombing). Tokyo: Iwanami Shoten, 1991.

Nagasaki City Board of Education, ed. *Nagasaki kyoryūchi: dentōteki kenzōbutsugun hozontaisaku chōsahōkokusho* (Nagasaki Foreign Settlement: Report on Measures for the Preservation of a Group of Traditional Buildings). Nagasaki, 1989.
----------. *Nagasaki koshashinshū kyoryūchihen* (Old Photographs of the Nagasaki Foreign Settlement). Nagasaki, 1995.
----------. *Higashiyamate, Minamiyamate no rekishitekiisan wo machizukuri ni ikasu tame ni* (Exploiting the Historic Assets of Higashiyamate and Minamiyamate in City-making). Nagasaki, 2004.

Nagasaki Prefecture, ed., *Nagasaki kyoryūchi gaikokujin meibo* (List of Foreign Residents of the Nagasaki Foreign Settlement). Nagasaki: Nagasaki Prefectural Library, 2004.

Nish, Ian, ed. *Britain & Japan: Biographical Portraits*. Folkestone, Kent: The Japan Library, 1994-1999.

Nishi-Nippon Heavy Industries Co. Ltd. Nagasaki Shipyard ed. *Mitsubishi Nagasaki zōsenjoshi zokuhen* (History of the Mitsubishi Nagasaki Shipyard. Nagasaki, 1951.

Noel-Paton, Ranald. *An Eastern Calling: George Windsor Earl and a Vision of Empire*. Bath: Ashgrove Publishing, 2018.

Paske-Smith, M. *Western Barbarians in Japan and Formosa in Tokugawa Days, 1603-1868*. Kobe: J.L. Thompson and Co., 1927.

Sakamoto Katsuhiko. *Meiji no ijinkan* (Foreign Houses of the Meiji Period). Tokyo: Asahi Shimbunsha, 1965.

Shigefuji Takeo. *Nagasaki kyoryūchi to gaikokushōnin* (Nagasaki Foreign Settlement and Foreign Merchants). Tokyo: Kazama Shobo, 1967.

Yamaguchi Mitsuomi. *Nagasaki no yōfū kenchiku* (Western-style Architecture in Nagasaki). Nagasaki: Nagasaki City Board of Education, 1967.

ABOUT THE AUTHOR

Brian Burke-Gaffney was born in Winnipeg, Canada in 1950 and came to Japan in 1972, going on to train for nine years as an ordained monk of the Rinzai Zen Sect. He left the monastery and moved to Nagasaki in 1982. He is currently professor emeritus of the Nagasaki Institute of Applied Science and honorary director of Glover Garden. He has published several books in Japanese and English, including *Starcrossed: A Biography of Madame Butterfly* (EastBridge, 2004) and *Nagasaki: The British Experience 1854-1945* (Global Oriental UK, 2009).

FLYING CRANE PRESS was established in 2015 to publish information in various formats on the history and culture of Nagasaki, Japan.

For information contact: flyingcranepress@yahoo.co.jp

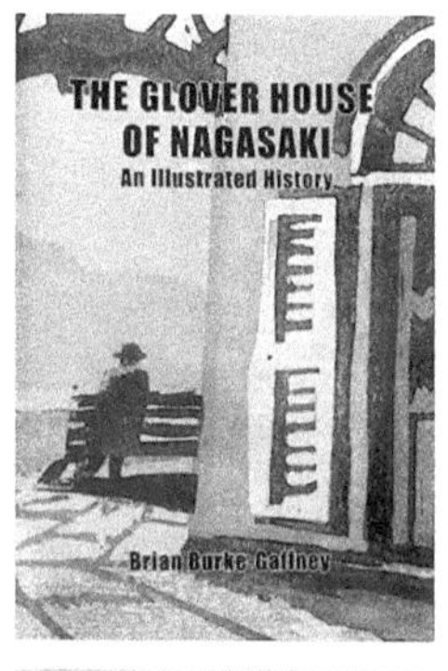

The Glover House of Nagasaki: An Illustrated History
Brian Burke-Gaffney
Nonfiction
English, 59 pages

The Nagasaki British Consulate, 1859-1955
Brian Burke-Gaffney
Nonfiction
English, 139 pages

Nagasaki: Tales of the Kataoka Houses
Brian Burke-Gaffney
Short story collection (fiction)
English, 205 pages

The Nagasaki Foreign Settlement:
People, Places, Stories
Lane R. Earns and Brian Burke-Gaffney
Nonfiction
English, 338 pages

The Road from Nagasaki to Unzen
Brian Burke-Gaffney
Nonfiction
English/Japanese, 188 pages